ROBIN HOOD

ROBIN HOOD:

ENGLISH OUTLAW

RICHARD DENHAM

Other titles by Richard Denham

The Britannia Trilogy

World of Britannia: Historical Companion to the Britannia Trilogy

Weird War Two

Weirder War Two

Arthur: Shadow of a God

CHAPTER ONE

THE GREENWOOD

'The Robin Hood story,' wrote Paul Vansittart in *Green Knights, Black Angels* (1969) 'has become a lament to a lost life. Can most readers at once distinguish glade, copse, thicket, grove, spinney, covert?'

The answer, of course, is that they cannot. Despite recent movements, like Friends of the Earth and Extinction Rebellion, which claim to be at one with nature, the green countryside that Robin would have known is largely unknown to most of us. Even those who live in country villages usually commute to the towns and cities for both work and relaxation.

Revellers in the May Day games (see Chapter Eight), with which Robin became inextricably associated by the Tudor period, often chanted this rhyme:

> 'O many one sings of grass, of grass,
> And many one sings of corn,
> And many one sings of Robin Hood
> Knows not where he was born.
>
> It was not in the Hall, the Hall,
> Nor in the painted bower,
> But it was in the good green-wood
> Among the lily flower.'

Wherever we believe Robin Hood lived (see Chapters Three and Thirteen) or even when (see Chapter Three) the common setting for the story is the greenwood; the forest. We are unused to such places today. Most of us live in an urban or semi-urban environment; when we go on holidays, we jet off to a place in the sun. Very few of us walk the bridle paths of England just for fun. This is, in part, because modern byelaws and an obsession with property ownership keep us out and in part because such forests have largely gone.

In the first systematic, though incomplete, survey of England, carried out by the commissioners of William I in 1086-7, about fifteen per cent of the country was covered in dense forest, often without any roads at all. Nowhere was more than five miles from woodland, although various areas of the north, Wales and Scotland were above the conventional tree line. The place names mentioned in the Domesday survey connected with woods have often survived – leah and hurst are the most common. Some of these woods dated from the Celtic, pre-Roman period. Others, like that which stood where

Stansted airport is today, grew after the Roman army abandoned Britannia in the early fifth century.

In Saxon and Norman England, some woodland was cleared to provide settlements, the traditional three field system that edged onto the woods that were kept both as sources of timber for dwellings and feeding places for pigs. In other areas, even where settlements were abandoned for whatever reason, the woodland grew again, hiding for centuries or perhaps for ever the evidence of man's existence.

Woods were often held as private property – estates came with a variable number of wooded acres. Equally often, they, along with the grassy common, were held by an entire community, so that everybody could take advantage of them. Property boundaries that edged forests were usually banks and ditches, what the Saxons called a wyrtruma, which is still visible occasionally today.

The trees themselves were oak, elm, ash, hazel, lime, hawthorn, maple and service. The only evergreens in England, highly relevant to the Robin Hood stories, were yew from which longbows were made. Old English woods, still in use when Robin is supposed to have lived, refer to different types of forest – fyrh, holt, scaga, wudu, bearu – but exactly what they mean and how they differed from each other is unknown today. It is a myth that a squirrel (red only, of course, in the Middle Ages) could travel from the Severn to the Wash without touching the ground, but a forest was the living embodiment of nature, which was not only a perfectly natural hiding place for an outlaw but almost had a life of its own.

As the *Readers' Digest Book of Folklore, Myths and*

Legends of Britain has it, 'The trees themselves whispered together, or roared angrily during the autumn gales; their longevity made a mockery of the life-span of puny men.' The Major Oak, for instance, in Robin Hood's Sherwood, is, according to dendro-chronologists, eight centuries old.

Trees therefore, in the age before Christianity, were believed to be gods themselves. Even the Christians could not shake off this notion entirely. Most of the Medieval ballads of Robin Hood (see Chapter Two) refer to 'him who dy'd by tre', in other words, Jesus Christ, crucified on a wooden cross. The Druids, the priests of the Celts, worshipped the oak, the rowan and the mistletoe, all of which could be found in Medieval woodland. Touching wood for good luck is almost all that remains now of ancestral tree-worship. The Christmas tree, a very late import into England and popularized by Prince Albert at Victoria's court and the traditional Yule log are reminders of it too and the maypole around which the King and Queen of the May danced, probably had its origins in ritual sacrifice.

Timber was essential in Robin Hood's time - all houses except the buildings of the Church or noble or royal castles, were made from timber, both for the framework (the traditional letter A shape) and the thin lattice slats for wattle and daub. All boats, from the little skiffs used on English rivers and lakes to the sea-going cogs and nefs were made from oak and elm.

The greenwood was traditionally the home of rabbits, hares, boar and deer and those were an important source of food for the poor until later centuries when the laws changed and such hunting was classed as poaching. In forests that belonged to the king, such as the New Forest in the south, the deer were also royal and the killing of them by other than royal hunting parties was punishable by death. This is very common in the older ballads of Robin Hood and the later ones that created the version we know today.

Despite this, the royal forests were shrinking in size by the early fourteenth century. The forest laws of 1306, drawn up by Edward I, perhaps the king on the throne in Robin's time, often gave way to local landowners and communities demanding their right to their use. Forest justices employed by the king appeared less regularly and had gone altogether by 1334. Private woodland, called Chases because deer and other animals were hunted there, was expanding in the same period. There was a landowner, Richard Hood, who was arguing with local foresters at Sowerby, Yorkshire in 1274. Forty years later, Robert Hood was paying for rights to firewood in Wakefield in the same county.

The bottom line was, whoever owned the forest and the game within it, they would defend it with every means at their disposal against the tyranny of outlaws and poachers.

The links with the forest were many and close. The term itself comes from an old Saxon term meaning 'fear' and even a horror movie as silly as *The Blair Witch Project* has the ability to remind us how terrifying an impenetrable wood can be. The jerky, hand-held camera was hailed as revolutionary at the time. As in all 'teen-slasher' movies, the sheer stupidity of the victims defies belief but the camera keeps returning to the swirling branches, the wind in the leaves, the crackling of the undergrowth. The forest is *alive*. There are no longer any English forests comparable with the Appalachian Trail described by Bill Bryson in *A Walk in the Woods* but there, every year, a number of people go missing by straying too far from the accepted paths. We have lost, if we ever had it, our native ability to navigate. On a different note, 'book' is derived from beech, because early writings were scratched on the bark strips torn from these trees.

There is a general belief that the yews found in many English churchyards today – supposedly to protect the dead from storms raised by witches – have much earlier Celtic connections. Until the eleventh century in various parts of Europe, it was illegal to own land which had been a tree sanctuary according to local legend. Many Irish and Welsh folktales have heroes like Son of Yew and Yew Berry and Iona itself, today's Anglesey, may be a corruption of oina – yewy. This was the headquarters of the Druids. Various yews have been dated by dendrochronologists and the results are surprising. One in Dyfed, Wales, at Flynnon Gwenlais dates from 500AD. At St Andrew's church, Compton Dunden in Somerset is another that is 1,700 years old.

The oak was a tree closely associated with the Celts and legend had it that cutting down an oak would result in it screaming and groaning in agony. The tree protected men from lightning. Carrying an acorn in a pocket preserved youth. A nail – or an arrow – driven into an oak tree was believed to be a sure-fire cure for toothache.

Apple trees had a sense of youth about them too; the Vikings who settled the north of England as the Danelaw which became Robin Hood's territory, brought this myth to England by the tenth century. Leaving an apple of a tree when the others had fallen or been picked presaged a family death. The ash tree cured rickets and hernias, especially in children whose little bodies were passed between branches which were then sealed with clay. The elder was a cursed tree. Not only was the 'true cross' on which Christ died traditionally made from it, but Judas Iscariot, the disciple who betrayed Him, hanged himself from an elder too, according to legend. The hazel was used by water diviners and searchers for buried treasure. In the particular case of Robin Hood, hazel wands were used both as targets and as objects magical and animate enough to point out thieves.

Holly kept out the evil eye and was an antidote to most poisons. Rowan or mountain ash was generally found, as it still is, in Scotland and the north. It was made into crosses worn around the neck to ward off evil and both the leaves and the berries were associated with successful births.

One of the most important trees which are linked with the stories of Robin Hood is the Trysting Tree. Apart from this, what is the relevance of the greenwood to the best known outlaw in British history? The prosaic answer is that a forest like Sherwood or Barnsdale, wherever our hero lived, could have provided shelter for a man or men on the run. We know that there were such outlaw bands in Medieval England (see Chapter Four) and when the pressure was on them from the authorities, it was the logical place to hide.

The earliest description of Robin from the ballads (see Chapter Two) is that he was a yeoman, a countryman of some social standing, below the middle class merchants of the towns but above the peasant freemen who were themselves above the lowly serfs. To put it into a rough modern context, he was at the top of the working class. The yeoman described by Geoffrey Chaucer in his 1380s *Canterbury Tales* is an attendant to the knight and his son the squire, the three of them in a company of thirty who are going on pilgrimage from the Tabard Inn in Southwark, London, to the shrine of Thomas Becket in Canterbury. Although Chaucer does not mention Robin Hood himself, it is interesting that his yeoman's chief skill should lie in hunting. He is a crack shot with a longbow, even though crossbows had long been used on the battlefield. Such men knew their local woods like the back of their hands and were able to disappear into their depths when required.

But the woodlands and Robin have another, far deeper, link. A man who wears green and lives in a forest. Camouflage? Common sense? Coincidence? Unlikely. One very strong possibility in our search for Robin Hood takes us in the direction of the darker side of the greenwood, to a realm of sorcerers, elves, fairies and the Medieval occult.

At a time when scholars were first beginning real research into who Robin Hood might have been and where his legend came from, Thomas Wright, one of the founders of the Camden Society in 1838, came out with the idea that 'Robin of the wood' 'belonged with tolerable certainty among the personages of the early mythology of the Teutonic peoples'. In other words, he was a Saxon tree spirit.

Another antiquarian, Joseph Hunter, challenged this view, complaining that Wright 'would represent the outlaw living in the woods as a mere creature of the imagination ... so far back that we know neither when nor where'. In other words, Hunter is saying that we cannot prove such a link, so it probably is not true. Can we do any better?

The Green Man is at once an artistic motif and the physical manifestation of a woodland spirit. If you walk in the woods, some people believe, you have a sense of someone watching you, walking with you or slightly behind; that is the green man. The term itself is very recent; it was coined by Julia, Lady Raglan, wife of the fourth earl, in an article she wrote for *The Folklore Journal* in 1939 and it caught on. The 1930s was a decade that saw renewed interest in the occult. There were poltergeist manifestations at Borley Rectory, the 'most haunted house in England' on the Suffolk/Essex border. Aleister Crowley, the 'great beast' was shocking society with his drug taking and promiscuous sex in the name of the devil. The Egyptologist Dr Margaret Murray formulated her idea that all kings of England up to Richard III who had met violent deaths were victims of ritual sacrifice. None of it made much sense, but the public were fascinated.

There is little doubt that the Green Man is an ancient fertility symbol and can be found in a number of cultures as far distant as Mogul India long before the Robin Hood stories. Oddly for a pagan deity, he can be found in a number of Christian churches, carved as a gargoyle or painted as frescos under the Puritan whitewash of the seventeenth century. He is another example of the Christians utilizing an existing faith and bolting it to their own. So the Roman Saturnalia, the Midwinter Solstice, became Christians celebrating Jesus' birth.

In reality, we have no idea when He was born, not even the exact year. Beltane, the Celtic festival of rebirth after the harshness of winter, became May Day, although paganism held on longest here, with the worship of the phallic maypole and the ritual dances of the Morris Men and even Robin Hood himself (see Chapter Eight).

It was perfectly acceptable, therefore, for the Green Man to be included in a pantheon of supernatural creatures which morphed over time into the devil.

There are three variants of the Green Man in Medieval art. The most common is the foliate version – a male face with hair and beard of leaves. Second – and this is the most common in England – is the disgorging head, in which vegetation spews forth from the Man's mouth, like a cornucopia of food. The oldest example of this can be found in France, at the church of St Hilaire Le Grande, dating to c.400AD. Tantalizingly, in one of the earliest ballads of Robin, Little John, his not-always-faithful sidekick, meets a young man in the woods and asks his name – 'Men call me Reynolde Grenelef' is the answer. Is Greenleaf the Green Man? Or is he Robin Hood himself?

The final version of the Green Man is the bloodsucker variant, foliage sprouting from mouth, nose, ears and eyes. In some incarnations, the face is depicted as a human skull, crawling with worm-like tendrils. Green Women are very rare, although some crypto-sociologists claim that they exist as fertility symbols without the foliage, usually with large breasts and genitalia.

It is probably impossible now to trace the origins of the Green Man. In Egyptology, he can be equated with Osiris, a vegetation deity associated with rebirth after his body was hacked to pieces. The Greeks called him Dionysius, a god linked with drunken orgies and the wild sexual debauches of Pan. The Romans, disapproving of Greek licentiousness, turned him into Bacchus, a drunken oaf perpetually inebriated with wine.

But there are other elements to all this. The Man has also been linked with Odin, father of the Norse gods, whose spelling of Woden takes us back to the woodland which is the eternal backdrop of the Robin Hood stories and the Teutonic theories of Thomas Wright. Odin is linked to Yggdrasil, the ash tree which in Norse mythology is the tree of life. In Celtic mythology, as we have seen, the ash, the yew and the oak were all sacred trees. From the eighth to the eleventh centuries, half England – the Danelaw – was controlled by Norsemen and their culture permeated Saxon society in the very areas, Nottinghamshire and Yorkshire, where Robin was supposed to have lived.

There are Green Man echoes in the horned god, Cernunnos to the Celts and Pan to the Romans, who may well be the male manifestation of fertility, the stag who is leader of the herd and the source of the next spring's crop of animals. As a god of the Old Religion, he became damned by the Christian church and morphed into the devil, complete not just with horns, but with cloven hoofs and a tail. In some parts of England, Cernunnos is Herne the Hunter, which brings us back yet again to the greenwood and the Medieval obsession with hunting. Herne was introduced as a seminal character in one of the best known television *Robins*, starring Michael Praed in 1984 (see Chapter

Twelve). The Wild Hunt is a Norse tradition, originally Odin and his hounds racing across the night sky. Those who saw the hunt or heard the braying of the hounds were marked for death. Herne is still said to haunt Windsor Great Park in Berkshire (the last claimed sighting was in 1962) and although modern folklore interpretations have made up a story set in the reign of any number of English kings, the stag-horned Herne is undoubtedly Cernunnos by a slightly different name.

Where, in all this, is Robin? According to etymologists, the name, itself a variant of the Norman Robert, comes from the Germanic/Saxon Hrodebert meaning bright or shining hood. The hood itself was a common form of headgear worn throughout the Middle Ages, superseded in the fifteenth century by a variety of caps. It was worn by both sexes and all classes as a protection against bad weather, but as a common item, it gave an outlaw a chance to blend with the crowd and to hide his face. Interestingly, the 'hoodie' fashion of the late twentieth century saw a re-emergence of this. Essentially a teenage item of clothing, it was equated by the older, more authoritarian elements of society with criminality, especially when gangs wore it irrespective of weather conditions. Whether any of this had any folk-memory of Robin Hood is difficult to say. In most Victorian and later depictions, Robin is rarely shown wearing his hood; the cap of estate, with pointed brim over the forehead, being far more usual.

He is Robin of the Greenwood and Green Robin. He is also Jack-in-the-Green and has certain similarities to the woodwose, the hairy wild men of the woods who were reported all over Europe from time to time and feature heavily in German heraldic motifs in the fourteenth to sixteenth centuries. In the Classical world, the woodwose was a satyr or faun, half man, half goat, usually shown with a huge erection and of course, the devil's cloven hoofs. It is first found as a surname – Woodhouse – in England in 1251.

But Robin Hood is also Robin Goodfellow, Shakespeare's Puck from *A Midsummer Night's Dream*. This mischievous fairy is much older than the sixteenth century, a spirit of the hearth that may have its origins in the Roman lares, the collection of household gods whose shrines in villas kept the house and household safe. A similar character is found in Norse mythology, Irish, Gaelic and so on, associated with pranks and practical jokes. The term hobgoblin means goblin (fairy) of the hearth and it is the kitchen which is Puck's home. The name Puck itself can be found in variants everywhere from Ireland to Finland and the term pixie is probably related to it.

Today, most historians have shared Joseph Hunter's view on Robin's link with the greenwood; he may have lived in it, but he was not mythologically part of it. There is nothing in the oldest written accounts of the outlaw, the ballads, which suggest the supernatural. We can make a strong case for King Arthur originally being a Celtic god, if only because virtually all his legends are steeped in magic. Robin Hood's are not.

So what do the oldest written sources tell us?

Richard Denham

CHAPTER TWO

THE RYMES OF ROBIN

HOOD

'If I shulde deye bi this day – we liste noughte to loke;
I can noughte ferfitly my pater-noster – as the prest it syngeth,
But I can rymes of Robyn hood …'

The character of Sloth in *The Vision of Piers Plowman*, written by William Langland c.1377 admits that his Lord's Prayer ('pater-noster') is imperfect – because he had only heard it in Latin in church and could not read it – but he did know the rhymes of Robin

Hood. This is clear evidence that by the late fourteenth century, Robin's existence was common knowledge. Whether that makes him a real, historical person of course is another question.

Langland, a tall, lugubrious churchman known as Long Will was probably in his forties when he wrote *Piers*. He was a clerk but could not take holy orders because he was married and made a living, appropriately enough (*Piers* is a gloomy, depressing story) chanting dirges at funerals. In his day, criticism of the Church was growing – funny, tongue-in-cheek examples of this can be found in Chaucer's *Canterbury Tales* written a few years after *Piers*. The message was clear – there was something scandalous and shameful about Sloth who preferred the layman's tales to holy writ. Thomas White, three hundred years later, was saying the same thing in his advice to children – 'When thou canst read, read no Ballads and foolish Books, but the Bible.'

The Gest of Robyn Hode

The longest and most detailed of the Medieval rhymes of Robin is *The Gest of Robyn Hode* which runs to nearly 14,000 words. It is clearly made up of at least three stories from different sources. 'Gest' does not mean 'joke', but comes from the Latin word *Gesta*, deeds. As we would say today, these are the adventures of Robin Hood.

Who was the *Gest* intended for? The answer lies in the first verse, but it raises more questions than it answers:

> 'Lythe [attend] and listen, gentilmen,
> That be of freborne [freeborn] blode,
> I shall you tel of a gode yeman,

His name is Robin Hode.'

'Gentlemen' was a relatively new term in the fourteenth century and had not yet been watered down to males generally. It applied to a status, probably of education and property, possibly even of title and 'freeborn' obviously cut out the serfs who were at the bottom of the heap of Medieval society. This group were, in effect, slaves; they had no rights in Medieval law and certainly not the education and literacy to read ballads like this.

The *Gest* tells us that Robin was a yeoman (see Chapter Fourteen) and even where he lived:

> 'Robyn stode in Bernesdale,
> And lenyd hym to a tre;
> And bi hym stode Litell Johnn,
> A good yeman was he.'

The only other two of the Merry Men are introduced next:

> 'And also dyd good Scarlok,
> And Much, the myller's son;
> There was non ynche of his bodi,
> But it was worth a grome [man]'

The exact relationship between them is not spelt out but John refers to Robin as 'Maister', so clearly he is the outlaw leader's inferior. Robin says he will not eat until John and the lads (the implication is that there are more of the band) walk up to 'the Saylis' (see Chapter Thirteen) and bring back a traveller to dine with them. To modern ears, this is taking hospitality a little far – 'inviting' somebody back to a forest for a meal with rough-looking strangers smacks of kidnapping. They do indeed find such a traveller, but not before Robin has warned them not to hurt a labourer, yeoman, knight or squire. The Church however are fair game:

> 'These bisshoppes and these archebisshoppes,
> Ye shall them bete and bynde,
> The hye sherif of Notyingham,
> Hym holde ye in your mynde.'

The greed and wealth of the Church were well known and clearly, the sheriff is Robin's *bête noire*. Various commentators have read a great deal into this. As we shall see, Robin changed considerably in the public consciousness over the centuries. Today he is a social rebel, stealing from the rich and giving to the poor, but he did not start out that way according to the ballads. In this verse, however, he says exactly what we expect – labourers, yeomen, knights and squires are good people; clerics and the sheriff are not. This is woefully wide of the mark. Much of the violence of the Middle Ages came precisely from the knightly class, who had the necessary weapons and military training to cause havoc. The concept of chivalry, to which modern Robin subscribes, was actually very superficial in most people, when supposedly noble knights like Richard I and Edward, the Black prince, were perfectly happy to put whole towns to the sword while on campaign.

    The traveller the outlaws find, looking pretty sorry for himself, is a shabbily dressed knight. He asks John who his master is and tells him he has heard of Robin Hood. The idea of master and man was a common one in Medieval society. It was strictly hierarchical from the king to the serf and most men, especially in a rural setting, would be likely to be someone's servant. Traditionally, they wore the livery of their masters, with coloured tunics and heraldic badges. They eat together and the knight confesses that he cannot pay for the meal. John checks his cloak and finds no money, so the knight explains his situation. The knight's son has killed another knight and his squire and, to buy the royal pardon for the crime, the knight has borrowed £400 (around £300,000 today) from the abbot of St Mary's in York (see Chapter Thirteen). If he cannot repay the loan, the knight will lose his land. Ever the generous outlaw, Robin offers the cash – which is, presumably, technically not his anyway, but stolen on the road. The knight has no guarantors other than 'Our Lady' (the Virgin Mary). This is fine with Robin, who also gives the knight a better horse, boots, clothes and spurs and sends him to York with John as his squire.

The theme of the Virgin Mary occurs frequently in the ballads. When they were written, almost certainly based on earlier, oral versions, England was wholly a Catholic country, nominally under the spiritual leadership of the pope. By the time a character called Robin Hood emerges in the Tudor May Day festivities, the country was going through seismic religious changes. Henry VIII's clash with the papacy over his divorce Catherine of Aragon led directly to England being placed under an interdict (barred from the benefits of the Church and from Heaven) and to the dissolution of the monasteries, at a stroke removing the avaricious monks whom Robin despised.

In York, the prior of St Mary's tells the abbot that the knight who owes them money is probably overseas. The implication here is that the knight is either on pilgrimage or crusade. In the case of the latter, he would already hold absolution from the pope for any crimes he may commit in the name of God (i.e. killing Muslims); in the former, knights usually went to Rome to obtain absolution (at a fee) for crimes already committed. Having prior *and* an abbot in St Mary's is confusing. An abbot presided over an abbey (which St Mary's was); a prior ran a smaller religious house (priory) altogether. This confusion almost certainly comes about because the *Gest* is a compilation of several stories.

The knight pays his dues, much to the annoyance of the St Mary's men who are after his land should he have failed to pay, and goes home to Wyresdale in Lancashire. On the way, there is a wrestling bout in which the knight saves a yeoman's life. This section or 'fytte' of the ballad does not concern Robin at all and may well have been shoehorned in from another story altogether. The wrestling match is an example of the inconsistency of the story and the social class from which Robin and his band came (see Chapter Fourteen). Wrestling, like quarter-staff fighting and football, was a 'working-class' sport. A knight would fight with a sword.

The forth fytte begins as the first, with Little John, Much and Scarlett sent off to find Robin a dining companion. To a modern readership this repetition is not only tedious but highly unlikely and it smacks of endless recent television series, both comedic and 'straight', where an artificial formula is the background to different stories. This time, the 'guest' is a monk, travelling in an entourage of more than fifty and with high quality packhorses. He is the high-cellarer of St Mary's and unlike the knight, who is impressed with Robin's reputation:

> '"He is a stronge thefe," said the monke
> "Of hym herd I never good".'

Under the threat of an arrow from Much's bow, the monk's companions vanish, leaving him with just a page and groom along with the packhorses. As high-cellarer at St Mary's, the monk has status and serious funds. Chaucer's monk in *The Canterbury Tales* owns two hunting dogs, a fine horse and wears boots of Spanish leather. This is, as we shall see in Chapter Five, a man who has vowed a life of poverty.

Whereas the knight was honest when asked how much money he carried, the monk lies about it after his meal in the greenwood. Robin claims that 'Our Ladye' [Heaven] has sent the monk (actually carrying £800 – over half a million in today's currency) to repay the loan to the knight. Then the knight arrives, having raised the money himself. Robin finally gives the knight half the monk's cash. These vast sums sound unlikely. No one carries that kind of cash today unless some shady drug or arms deal is involved. When the ballads were written however, banking as we know it did not exist and wealthy travellers may choose to carry their worldly goods with them rather than risk leaving them behind. King John famously lost his crown jewels (in reality, his war chest of cash) in the Wash near Lincoln during his war with the barons in 1216. The large amount the monk is carrying explains the size of his retinue, even if, scared off by one bowman, they may not have been the right men for the job!

The story is frankly scrappy, with a number of loose ends and unexplained situations, but presumably, a relatively simplistic audience, of peasant or yeoman class, would not ask too many questions and if Langland's Sloth knew these verses (all 456 of them that make up the *Gest*!) there was a monotonous comfort in the re-telling that transcended the mistakes and lack of coherent storyline.

The second part of the *Gest* focuses on the eternal villain, the Sheriff of Nottingham. The man's writ could not actually have extended as far north as Barnsdale (in Yorkshire) because although Barnsdale and Sherwood are only forty miles apart, that was two days' journey in the fourteenth century. It is Little John, not Robin, who takes part in an archery contest and so impresses the sheriff that he offers John a place in his entourage. This theme, of archery contests and men invited into service, is a common theme of those early ballads.

John behaves as a complete scoundrel while serving the sheriff, lying in bed for hours, quarrelling with other staff and eventually scuttling off with £300 and the sheriff's family silver! John lures the sheriff into the forest (Sherwood is actually mentioned nowhere) on the pretext of a hunt and the sheriff ends up dining with Robin Hood off his own silver. Stripped of his fine clothes, he is released on his assurance that he will, in future, leave the outlaws alone.

Not content with one archery contest, the *Gest* now has another, probably because this is from a different tale altogether and Robin, John and a third character – 'Gilbert with the white hand' – are all crack shots. This is much more like the varieties of the story that we are familiar with from Hollywood (see Chapter Twelve). The whole thing is an ambush and Little John is wounded, the outlaws escaping to a castle near Nottingham owned by Sir Richard at the Lee, a friendly knight. Rather bizarrely, the sheriff goes to London to inform the king of these events – exactly why is not explained. On his way back he takes Sir Richard prisoner and Robin rescues him, wounding the 'proude sherif' with an arrow before killing him with his sword:

> 'Lye thou there, thou proude sherife,
> Evyl mote thou cheve [evilly must you die]
> There might no man to the triste
> The whyles thou were a lyve.'

This second part is even more of a mish-mash than the first, clearly taken from a number of different stories which are not Robin-related at all. We have no idea whether Sir Richard here is the same as the anonymous knight in the ballad's first section.

The third part sees the king, now called Edward, arrive in person with an armed retinue to sort the outlaws out. This has no precedent in actual history. Although *very* occasionally the king might try a case himself rather than leave the matter with his travelling justices, he was unlikely to act as policeman rounding up felons. The action however has spread to Lancashire and specifically 'Plomton Parke' (near Knaresborough in Yorkshire). A forester suggests that the best way to find Robin Hood is to go undercover as a monk, which he does and sure enough, the outlaw finds him and relieves him of half his cash, letting him keep the rest. There is another archery contest (!) during which Robin at last recognises the king:

> 'And so dyde all the wylde outlawes,
> Whan they se them knele;
> "My lorde the kynge of Englande,
> Now I knowe you well".'

This too is a common feature of later movies, when Richard the Lionheart returns from crusade, but it raises the interesting side issue of just how recognizable a Medieval king was. Other than a handful of portraits in royal or lordly households, the only visual record of a king was on coins of the realm and these were woefully unrealistic. We have no information in the ballads of Robin's background – he is not yet referred to as the Earl of Huntington, for example – so he would have no yardstick by which to measure the king's appearance. The king accepts Robin's grovelling adulation, all part of the divine aspect of kingship, and grants him a place at court. Robin agrees and brings along his Merry Men too – not the tiny handful we know by name, but 'seven score and three' – in other words, all 143 of them!

In the last section, time has passed and Robin has lived in the king's service for over a year. He longs to go back to the greenwood and only John and Will Scarlett are still with him. The king grants him a week's leave but once back in Barnsdale, Robin cannot bear to go back to court. He lives for over twenty years in the forest until he is betrayed by a relative of his, the prioress of Kirklees who is in cahoots with another villain, Roger of Doncaster.

The unnamed prioress ticks all the boxes of a Medieval villainess. First, she is female, as weak and treacherous as Eve, responsible, according to the Old Testament, for all man's woes. Second, she is a member of the greedy and tricksy Church that Robin despises. Third, as a noble hero, he cannot simply die in battle (and certainly not of an age-related illness); he must be a victim of treachery. The prioress, incidentally, has no qualms in having what appears to be a sexual liaison with Roger of Doncaster and they kill Robin (exactly how, the ballad does not tell us) when he attends the priory 'to be leten blode'. Blood-letting was a well-established Medieval cure for all sorts of ailment. It relied on cleansing the body and balancing the four humours which made the body function. Someone in a weakened state from temporary blood loss was a sitting duck:

> 'Cryst have mercy on his sole,
> That dyed on the rode [cross]
> For he was a good outlawe,
> And dyde pore men moch god.'

This last line is the only one in the early ballads that hints at the now-conventional looking after the poor by stealing from the rich. Cash redistribution like this is highly unlikely, but of course that is what makes Robin Hood stand out. There is no evidence from the ballads as to *how* he did poor men much good, so we are very much in the dark about the outlaw's other exploits.

Robin Hood and the Monk
The mid-fifteenth century *Monk* ballad is, in many

ways, the best of the rhymes of Robin Hood. Much shorter than the *Gest*, it was probably written to be recited, not sung by a troubadour, the wandering minstrels who made their reputation in the royal courts of England from the twelfth century onwards.. We do not actually know what his ballad was called when it was written – the *Monk* title was not given to it until 1832. It contains several mini-stories; a parody on knightly virtues (*The Tournament at Tottenham*); and *The Clerk and the Nightingale*, a discussion on women. Because of this, the anonymous author may well have been a clerk himself, though probably not in holy orders.

The ballad opens with:

'In somer, when the shaws be sheyne
And leves be large and long,
Hit is full mery in feyre foreste
To here the foulys song.'

'Shawes be sheen' means 'the woods are bright' and this is a standard opening of several Medieval poems, reflecting the fascination with the greenwood we saw in Chapter One. Chaucer's *Canterbury Tales* from seventy years earlier has a similar start, extolling the virtues of the season (April in Chaucer's case), the bursting greenery and the singing birds. It is all very idyllic and of course we are straight away in dales and hills and the 'grene wode tre'. Interestingly, Little John, who opens the narrative, comments on what a lovely day it is 'Be hym that dyed on tre'; in other words, Christ, crucified on a wooden cross.

Robin, as a good Christian, bemoans the fact that he has not been able to attend Mass for a fortnight and Much suggests that he goes with twelve armed men at his back. Although open air services probably were held from time to time (the call to arms by Pope Urban II that led to the First Crusade in 1095 had to be held outside a church because of the size of the congregation) the usual pattern was to hold Mass inside. All services were in Latin – the pater-noster sung by the priest – and the worshippers prayed lying face down on the flagstone floor. There were no pews in Medieval churches. Robin agrees to take just Little John and the pair take part in an archery contest which John wins. This is the second time we have seen Robin's lieutenant as a better shot than he is and the rivalry between them is a constant theme in most of the Robin stories. They quarrel and Robin goes on to Nottingham alone while John returns to Sherwood.

He prays in St Mary's church but a monk recognises him and tells the sheriff that 'the kynggis felon' is in town. Clearly, there is personal spite in this – Robin once stole £100 from the monk (who, of course, as a churchman should never have owned that much in the first place). The sheriff's men arrive and a fight breaks out (sacrilegious, of course, inside a church). A clue that this is a fifteenth century ballad lies in the mention of Robin's 'too-hond sworde'. This was probably a 'bastard' or 'hand a half' weapon, nearly four feet long and heavier than the standard broadsword. From the 1450s onwards, fencing schools, especially in Germany, taught the use of such weapons. Robin kills twelve of the sheriff's men and wounds more, but his sword breaks when he clashes with the sheriff himself.

There must be a missing section here (parts of the original manuscript are damaged by damp) because we are suddenly in Sherwood with the outlaws hearing of Robin's capture. Presumably feeling guilty, John decides to rescue his leader and Much joins him. On the way, they meet a monk (as always, a rascal) and when he tells them he is glad that Robin has been captured, John loses his cool and beats the man up, dragging him from the saddle. Much kills the monk's page and they bury them both without a marker.

The casual violence in the ballads would not have upset the first listeners/readers, any more than television blood and gore offends most of us today. Violent death was a way of life in the Middle Ages. Criminals were hanged in public. Fights broke out often. *Every* male carried a knife. Traitors' heads were impaled on spikes on top of gates or castle walls. Nobody laments the murder of the monk and the page (who would only have been a boy) – life was too nasty and short for all that.

There is now another break and we are suddenly with the king. John gives his lord letters carried by the monk (we do not know what they contain) and the king employs both men who carry the royal seal back to the sheriff. The use of a seal was the mark of authenticity in the Middle Ages. Despite the continuing error in far too many books, King John did not *sign* Magna Carta in 1215, he *sealed* it. There were several royal seals, from the Great Seal to the signet, all of them being the royal arms, which only the king and his officials had access to. They find the town gates of Nottingham barred because Robin Hood is imprisoned inside but John gains access to the sheriff anyway and passes the royal letters to him. When the sheriff asks where the monk, the original carrier of the letters is,

John tells him that the king has made him abbot of Westminster. While the extraordinarily trusting sheriff is sleeping off a liquid dinner, John sneaks into the gaol (almost certainly in Nottingham castle), kills the guard and rescues Robin.

The sheriff is furious and realises that he has been duped, sending out men in all directions even though the outlaws are already by now hiding safely in Sherwood. The king is aware that John has scammed him, but he writes it off because John's fealty to his master Robin is greater than to him and, very reasonably, under the circumstances, he understands that:

'Thus endys the talking [poem] of the munke
And Robyn Hode I wysse [indeed]
God, that is ever a crowned king,
Bryng us all to his blisse!'

Robin Hood and the Potter

The title was given to this ballad by the antiquarian Joseph Ritson who collected this and other Medieval works in a portfolio in 1795. Because of the lines which appear just before the *Potter* in the original version, we can date it to about 1503. Reference is made to 'exspences of fflesche at the marriage of my ladey Margaret, that sche had owt off Eynglonde'. The flesh refers to meat – in other words, this is a butcher's bill – for the food consumed at the wedding of Henry VII's daughter Margaret to the Scottish king James IV on 8 August 1503 at Holyrood Abbey, Edinburgh.

The text of the original is repetitious and carelessly copied, making the sense of it more difficult than the other two ballads we have met so far. Part of this is dialect, spellings that are usually found in the Midlands, which might tell us something about the original writer (or copyist) but not necessarily anything about Robin Hood. English spelling is a constantly changing subject. What was once called the queen's English, as written and spoken by the BBC in the middle of the twentieth century, has all but disappeared under a deluge of Americanisms, not helped by the fact that the subject is now thought relatively unimportant in schools. What we have in the ballads is a reminder that there were no rules in the fifteenth century and the same word can be spelled differently in a single passage or even sentence. Because there are various references to yeomen as the audience of this ballad, we can be fairly certain that this was the class the poet aimed at; Robin was a yeoman – he was one of their own.

In the *Potter*, it is, surprise, surprise, summer again. The birds are singing and there is blossom everywhere. A 'proud potter' turns up (pride being seen as a sin long before the Puritans hijacked it in the sixteenth century) and Little John has a score to settle with the man; he beat him, perhaps at a wrestling match, at Wentbridge (see Chapter Thirteen). He bets Robin – and anybody else among the Merry Men - that they cannot make the potter pay the going rate for passage through the greenwood. Sure enough, the potter is not having any of Robin's intimidation and they fight, the outlaw's sword and buckler to the potter's quarter-staff. Robin loses to him and says he will go to Nottingham to sell the potter's pots. Again, this is a contrived situation. There is no need for Robin to impersonate the potter, but the notion of disguise was popular at all levels of society. We even find it, improbably, in Shakespeare's *Merchant of Venice* when Portia appears as a (male) lawyer to demand justice from the 'harsh Jew' Shylock.

No sooner said than done, the outlaw ends up in the town's market place, crying his wares and is soon surrounded by wives and widows. Clearly, Robin is no salesman. Pots that were worth five pence, he ends up selling for three. Even the sheriff's wife buys from him and invites him to eat with them. It is not long before an archery contest is arranged – although why a potter should also be a crack shot is not discussed. The contest itself is the most detailed in any Robin ballad, the bullseye in the target's centre being a wooden block called a prick.

The sheriff is lured into the greenwood and the potter reveals himself as Robin Hood, having sounded his horn to summon the Merry Men. The sheriff is allowed to go and returns to Nottingham with only his horse. Throughout the ballad are hints that Robin and the sheriff's anonymous wife are having some sort of flirtation. He gives her a gold ring and a horse and she, by definition, offers him hospitality when he is still disguised as the potter. She colludes in the sheriff's embarrassment:

> 'With that shce take up a lowde lawhyng
[laughing]
>> And swhare be hem that dyed on tre,
>> Now haffe you payed for all the pottys
>> That Robin gaffe to me.

The later ballads of Robin Hood cannot be said to be Medieval, dating as they do from the late sixteenth or even seventeenth century. They are all part of the enduring legend of the outlaw however and we will discuss them in a later chapter.

CHAPTER THREE

THE BOY'S OWN ROBIN

(AND THE REALITY)

In December 1819, the poet and novelist Walter Scott published his tenth Waverley novel, *Ivanhoe*. It was the first one set in England (as a Scot, Scott had set the others north of the border) and easily the most successful. It was hugely popular, written at a time when all things Medieval were finding a new fascination for the public. Five different dramatizations wowed audiences in 1820 alone. One of the set-pieces of the novel is a tournament at Ashby-de-la-Zouche, so one of the productions was put on at Astley's amphitheatre in

London, which normally put on pageants, parades and equestrian events. Twenty mounted knights took part.

The story is a classic. Set in the reign of Richard the Lionheart, it features the hero, Wilfred (!) of Ivanhoe, cruelly disinherited by his stern, unbending father. Ivanhoe loves the gorgeous, blonde Rowena. Together they are the perfect couple but Fate stands in the way of their happiness. Ivanhoe's father is under attack from the dastardly minions of Prince John, running England (badly) in Richard's absence on crusade. First among these is the treacherous Brian de Bois-Guibert, a Templar who is also in love with Rowena. The Templars still have a bad press today, despite the attempts by historians to rehabilitate them. Originally set up, along with the Hospitallers, to protect Jerusalem from the Infidel, these warrior-monks became hugely wealthy and powerful, ending with their destruction by the French king Philip IV in 1314.

Ivanhoe himself spends most of the book recovering from his tournament wounds and he is helped by Isaac of York, a Jew whose daughter Rebecca falls in love with Ivanhoe. This relationship is doomed to failure because of the Medieval attitudes to Jews (see below). Even in Walter Scott's day, Jews were unpopular, easily turned into villains like Fagin by Charles Dickens some years later. They could not stand for parliament until 1858.

To Ivanhoe's aid, too, comes Robin of Loxley and his Merry Men who live in Sherwood Forest. The story ends with Ivanhoe killing Bois-Guibert and King Richard coming back to claim his throne, granting Robin's outlaws a full pardon in the process.

All the later stories, as opposed to original ballads which are very different, follow this line, as do most film and television treatments. We shall look at the origins of this, from which Scott drew his inspiration, later.

The sanitized, boys' own version of history, taught in all British schools throughout the first three quarters of the twentieth century and which is surprisingly difficult to shake off, goes something like this.

Richard I is a natural hero. Tall, good-looking and probably blond, he wants to fulfil the destiny of any Christian king by winning back the Holy Land and particularly Jerusalem from the dastardly Turks who not only regarded Jerusalem as *their* holy city but had the nerve to capture it *and* to destroy a Christian army in 1187. This is how the average naïve reader of Walter Scott saw it and countless readers of later children's versions. While he is away on crusade, he leaves the government of his kingdom to his little brother John, who is everything Richard is not. He is treacherous, spineless and deceitful and cannot wait to get his hands on real power.

Aiding and abetting him, at least in the Nottinghamshire area, is the Sheriff of that county. Children growing up in the 1950s when *Robin Hood* was a weekly staple diet of entertainment on the television (see Chapter Twelve), equated sheriff with good guy, the star-wearing gunfighter of the westerns they also watched. For reasons that made little sense to the young and uninitiated, this particular sheriff was a baddie.

He routinely taxed the downtrodden peasantry and sent his Norman-helmeted thugs to beat up anybody who crossed him. Enter Robin of Loxley, an upright, true-blue Englishman in the Richard mould who found himself outlawed when he stood up to the sheriff's misdeeds. Hiding in Sherwood Forest, while trying to maintain an on-off relationship with his girlfriend, Maid Marian, he set up a group of trusty, like-minded freedom fighters, among whom are Little John, Will Scarlett, Friar Tuck, Mutch the Miller's Son and (because songs were still part of rattling good television yarns in the 1950s) a troubadour, Alan a Dale. This Merry band crossed the sheriff at every turn until that glorious day when King Richard returned from crusade and kicked both John and the sheriff into touch. Ah, different days!

Now, let us look at the reality. Richard was crowned on 2 September 1189 at Westminster Abbey, as was traditional for English kings. This was his own personal fiefdom or demesne, private lands, which explains the rather odd siting of his Victorian statue outside the Houses of Parliament that did not exist in his day.

The previous six years had been tempestuous when all three surviving sons of Henry II – Richard, Geoffrey and John – squabbled with each other and with their father over who should succeed him. The rule of primogeniture – the right of the eldest to rule – had yet to be formulated. Richard, known in his lifetime as Oc e No (Yes or No) was renowned for keeping his word. If he said Yes, he meant it; likewise, No. And his word, in 1189, was a determination to go on crusade.

The role of a king in the Middle Ages was twofold, as the coins of their reigns showed. On the obverse, the king sat in splendour on his throne, the orb in one hand, the sceptre in the other. He was dispenser of justice, arbiter of disputes, defender of the Church. On the reverse, he was a warrior, mounted in full armour, a general and war-leader of his country. In Richard's case, he took the second role more seriously than the first.

There had already been two crusades to take and keep Outremer, the Holy Land centring on Jerusalem, but by 1189 the city had fallen to the Seljuks (not actually Turks at all, but Syrians), commanded by one of the most iconic of Islam's leaders, Salah-ed-Din, who would become Richard's nemesis. Joining forces with his cousin, Philip II of France, Richard left England in July 1190. Dynastic squabbles broke out almost at once, Richard fighting a mini-war against Tancred of Sicily, thereby boosting the size of his campaign chest but failing to marry, as he had promised, Philip's sister Alys, to whom he had been betrothed when they were children. While Richard's formidable mother, Eleanor of Aquitaine, brought in another wife, the Spanish princess Berenegaria of Navarre, Philip stormed off in a huff for the Holy Land, leaving Richard behind.

In catching up, Richard clashed with Isaac Comnenus, the ruler of Cyprus, took the island and sold it to Guy de Lusignan, the exiled king of Jerusalem, who had lost his crown and city four years earlier. Finally reaching his destination, Richard took the sea port of Acre which had been under siege for two years, supposedly insulting his ally, Leopold of Austria, by comparing his battle-flag to a dishcloth! Leopold and Philip both went home, leaving Richard to it and, incidentally, condemning the Third Crusade to failure.

The king defeated Salah-ed-Din at Arsuf but Jerusalem proved too tough a nut to crack. Looking at the city today, its Medieval walls do not seem particularly impregnable, but the English army was reduced, especially due to disease and the heat and Richard concluded a truce with the Muslims which effectively left the city in their hands.

Despite the ultimate failure of his goal, Richard's military reputation soared. He was seen, and not just in England, as a conquering hero. As Duke of Normandy and owner of over a third of France, he had a huge following across the Channel too.

The voyage home however was perilous. Sea journeys were always dangerous and Richard's ship was wrecked in the Adriatic, meaning that he had to travel by land. That took him through the territories of Leopold of Austria who was bent on revenge for Richard's slur at Acre. The king was disguised, in true Robin Hood tradition, as a woodsman, but his expensive gloves gave him away and he was imprisoned for fifteen months while negotiations continued for his ransom to be paid to Leopold's overlord, the Holy Roman Emperor, Heinrich VI.

What of the other aspect of Richard's rule, the care of his kingdom? Laying aside the likelihood that he may have been psychotic and probably homosexual (traits that only a select few would know about and would *never* feature in any Robin Hood story) the whole reign had begun badly. In July 1189, against the wishes of the establishment, Richard declared a general amnesty of criminals, releasing hundreds from various prisons all over the country. The chronicler William of Newburgh wrote, 'Through the king's clemency, these pests came forth from prison, perhaps to become bolder thieves in the future.' Was Robin Hood among them?

Worse still was a pogrom that took place on the day of Richard's coronation. Jews all over Europe had been attacked from time to time, accused of the ritual slaughter of Christian children. They had been told explicitly to stay away from the coronation festivities, but they came anyway. There was a sudden burst of violence and hundreds of Jews were butchered before the new king could put a stop to it all. By the time 300 of them were burned in the Clifford Tower in York, Richard had left the country and the Jews to their fate.

Despite the fact that Richard had a soft spot for John and would forgive him anything, he perhaps realized that leaving him to govern as regent would be a disaster. Richard was going to war, with all the perils that that entailed and might not come back. Accordingly, he left William de Mandeville, Earl of Essex and Hugh Puiset, Bishop of Durham, as justiciars, ruling in his place. The more redoubtable William Longchamps, Earl of Surrey, replaced them.

To keep John out of the way, Richard gave him carte blanche of five counties in Normandy, but that did not satisfy the youngest of the Plantagenets, who was more petulant than Richard and had none of his redeeming qualities of generosity and courage. As soon as Richard had left England, John was back, making life difficult for the justiciars and feathering his own nest where he could. He had been granted six English counties too but that was not enough for John. He was sceptical, cynical, anti-church and a feeble general. Generations of historians have failed to rehabilitate him, partly because the PR job on Richard has been so good and, although they would never admit it, partly because of Walter Scott's version of the Robin Hood legend.

Annoyed by William Longchamps' French attitudes (the man was from Normandy) John determined to bring him down. His army took London and he bribed the citizens by letting them elect their own mayor, which they have done ever since. By the end of October 1191, Longchamps had gone. Living up to the nickname 'Lackland' that his father had given him because as a youngest son, there were no territories left to dole out, John concluded a treaty with Philip of France whereby he gave away vast swathes of Normandy. It is difficult to see what, apart from a reputation for sheer stupidity, John or England got out of this.

John's arrogance and high-handed treatment of his people grew infinitely worse once he was king, but that takes the Robin Hood story into another, unrelated, phase. The raising of taxes which is a common complaint in the post-Walter Scott era of Robin, may be associated with the need to raise a vast sum – 150,000 marks – to secure Richard's release from Leopold's prison. England had already been screwed by the Saladin Tithe, increased taxation to fund the Third Crusade itself.

Richard's return to England was not the happy ending we associate with, for example, dear old Sean Connery riding into the greenwood at the end of *Robin Hood: Prince of Thieves* (1991). John must have had a certain charm because Richard forgave him and presumably those supporters like the fictional sheriff of Nottingham who had caused such grief to Richard's poor subjects.

The bottom line in the Nottingham Richard version is that, as always in real history, nothing is black and white. Richard was not a 'good' king any more than John was a 'bad' one. Of the ten years of his reign, Richard spent less six months of it in England. He never went on a royal tour to meet his people. He made no laws (unlike his father, Henry II) for their benefit. He probably could not even speak their language. As for John, he is guilty of a great deal, but most of this was *after* his accession to the throne in 1199 and has nothing to do with Robin Hood. His most grievous 'crime' was in trying to bring the greedy barons of England to book after they themselves had wilfully extended their powers in the king's absence while Richard was on crusade.

This led to his famous sealing of Magna Carta, perhaps the most over-rated document in Medieval history. Like the American Declaration of Independence, written over five centuries later, it is full of holes in terms of logic. It was not, as some commentators have contended, a blueprint for democracy, but merely sixty-three whinges about John's supposed misuse of power. The truth is that the barons themselves had taken advantage of Richard's absence to increase their power at the expense of the king's. Within weeks of sealing it, John had effectively torn up Magna Carta and the pope of the day, the brilliant Innocent III, declared the document null and void anyway.

So far we have looked at the reality of politics against the background of Walter Scott's fictional knight Ivanhoe and, unsurprisingly, it does not match up. Another Robin, the possible historical figure from Yorkshire rather than Nottinghamshire, has no exact parallel because there is no 'boys' own' version. No one of Scott's literary stature has come up with a sanitized hero in Henry III's or Edward I's reign, so we can only look at the reality of what went on.

There are two texts which place Robin in a slightly later period than Scott's. The first is from *Scotichronicon*, written by the chronicler John of Fordun between 1377 and 1384 and revised by Walter Bower in 1440. Bower was particularly dismissive of those who liked the stories of 'Robertus Hode and Littell Johanne', calling them 'stolidum vulgus', stupid people. From the context of Fordun's account, the 'then' refers to 1266:

> 'Then arose a famous murderer, Robert Hood, as well as Little John, together with their accomplices from among the disinherited …'

Twenty years after Bower, an anonymous monk wrote:

> 'Around this time according to popular opinion, a certain outlaw named Robin Hood, with his accomplices, infested Sherwood and other law-abiding areas of England with continuous robberies.'

Interestingly, in this version, now kept in Eton College's library, there is no mention of Yorkshire and we are back in Sherwood.

From these three chroniclers – Fordun, Bower

and the anonymous monk – we can actually place an historical Robin in the 1260s and 1270s, whereas he is totally missing from the historical record in the reigns of Richard and John.

So what was happening in the 1260s to make 'Robert Hood' rise up? The king by this time was Henry III who first came to the throne as a nine year old boy in 1216, after the death of his father, John. Another civil war was raging in the country then as the royal faction (John's followers) fought the barons after the king had effectively reneged on the agreement known as Magna Carta the previous year. The justiciars who ruled during Henry's minority, William Marshal and Hubert de Burgh, defeated the rebels and ensured that the young king's coronation took place. Not until 1227 would Henry rule in his own right.

In a trend that would be repeated in later years, Henry appointed a variety of Frenchmen to key posts in his court. He married a French princess, Eleanor Berenger of Provence, and everything French – the music, fashions and courtly romances of, for example, King Arthur – became fashionable. This included an expensive rebuilding programme of castles and cathedrals in the (French) Gothic style.

The losers in this trend were the English barons. Henry was in effect ignoring Magna Carta nearly as much as John had and hit them with high taxation, particularly scutage, the 'shield tax' that was nominally to pay for war; except that Henry fought no wars, preferring to negotiate with the kings of Scotland and princes of Wales instead. He was also giving away English lands in France to avoid conflict.

The 'Mad' parliament in Westminster in 1258

brought all this to an end – of sorts. Parliament is actually a misnomer for this group. They were merely the king's great council, composed entirely of Lords and senior churchmen, but they drew up a charter, the Provisions of Oxford, which tried to reduce Henry's arbitrary appointment of his foreign favourites. True to form, the king ignored this too and by 1264 civil war had broken out again.

This time the baronial rebels had a real leader, but he was as high-handed and self-centred as Henry and was the king's brother-in-law, Simon de Montfort, precisely one of those foreigners who had been ennobled by the king who had made him Earl of Leicester. The Welsh prince Llewellyn ap Gruffydd, ever eager to extend his own territory, took de Montfort's side and Henry, no general it has to be said, was defeated at Lewes on 14 May. The king was forced to call a parliament. This one, which met in 1265, is the first that equates, however roughly, with the modern structure. De Montfort was no democrat but he realised that wealthier members of the common people (by which he meant the land-owning upper middle class) should have a say in government. Henry's successor, Edward I, who may be the 'king Edward' referred to in the early Robin Hood ballads, agreed. 'Quid omnes tangit, ab omnibus approbetur' (that which affects all, should be decided by all) was a precept of his reign.

In 1265, Henry was de Montfort's prisoner and had little choice but to agree to the rebels' demands. His son Edward – 'as brave and as treacherous as the leopard' which was his coat of arms – was a prisoner too but he escaped and his army defeated de Montfort's in a loop of the river

Avon near Evesham. The rebel leader was killed, duped by Edward who literally used false flags to lull de Montfort into believing that reinforcements were coming to his aid from Kenilworth.

By 1297, Henry had been ruling for over fifty years and he was losing his grasp. Effectively, from that year, Edward acted as regent, while the king focussed on the remodelling of Westminster Abbey.

Exactly what part, if any, the historical Robin Hood plays in all this can only be guesswork. In the ballads, the king (Edward) is a one-dimensional figure with no character at all, so that is unhelpful. Whereas Walter Scott had Robin of Loxley fighting manfully against the injustices of Prince John's government, there is simply no information about him in the 1260s. As an outlaw, we might believe that he fought under de Montfort, perhaps at Evesham, where he would have been lucky to escape alive. Every Medieval army had contingents of longbowmen, so it is not unreasonable to assume that Robin, accomplished archer that he was, should have joined the levies on one side or the other.

The wider implications are more difficult. Because there was civil war in England in the 1260s, does that mean that there was chaos with families torn apart according to their principles? Emphatically not. There *are* examples of this in the seventeenth century civil war, when politics was far more to the front, but in the thirteenth century, it is unlikely that the ordinary man was much bothered by events at court. The geography of the barons' war all happened miles from Robin's supposed centre in Yorkshire, so depredations by marauding armies were not likely to be an issue.

But there is a possible 'third Robin Hood

which almost pales into insignificance beside the other two. Some commentators argue that the 'comely [handsome] king Edward' of the ballads, is not Edward I, but his son, Edward of Caernarfon, who became the first Prince of Wales and later Edward II.

Edward I was busy subduing the Welsh at the time, building the circle of magnificent castles like Caernarfon, Harlech and Beaumaris, which still stand. The story that he held the infant Edward up on a shield on a castle rampart to show the Welsh people what they wanted – 'a prince who can speak no English' – is the kind of fabrication that Walter Scott might have been guilty of!

Edward II, like John, is still an unpopular king in the eyes of the public. Wedged between a warrior father and a warrior son (Edward III) he was not much of a soldier and his homosexuality meant that he had passions for foreign noblemen, like Piers Gaveston, to whom he gave estates and power. In that sense, what we have with Edward is a repetition of events under Henry III and the result was the same – another war with the barons. His own wife, Isabella, the 'she-wolf of France', turned against him and plotted his murder with her lover, Roger Mortimer, Earl of March. When Edward Prince of Wales became Edward III in 1330, he immediately dissolved his mother's regency and executed Mortimer. The king himself was murdered at Berkley Castle in Gloucestershire on the orders of Isabella and Mortimer, according to legend by having a red-hot poker inserted into his rectum.

It is not possible to find Robin Hood in Edward II's tortuous reign. In a time of weak government and instability – as with Richard I's

absence and Henry III's clash with the barons –
crime and lawlessness tend to increase and certainly,
we know from the historical record, that there seems
to have been a crime wave in the 1330s, focussing
on highway robbery (see Chapter Four). The rest is
silence.

Robin Hood is such an enigmatic character that it is
not easy to see him in the historical record of any of
the periods in which he is presumed to have lived.
One thing is certain, however. The very lack of
historical records must mean that Robin's social
status was indeed yeoman. Any member of the
gentry – as in Robin of Loxley – would have
featured, surely, in some paperwork somewhere.

CHAPTER FOUR

THE MERRY MEN?

Little John, Will Scarlett, Mutch the Miller's Son, Alan a Dale. We quickly run out of names for Robin's outlaw band who made their home in Sherwood or Barnsdale or wherever else they could escape the authorities. If we add Friar Tuck to this mix as some sort of chaplain or spiritual guide, we only have a gang of five. The main rivals of Robin Hood (see Chapter Nine) were only three, yet the followers of various worldwide and much later Robin wannabees run into the hundreds (see Chapter Eleven).

Practically speaking, for an outlaw gang to exist undetected in remote countryside and remain one step ahead of the law, the smaller the number the better. Simply accommodating and feeding large numbers would cause huge logistical problems and increase the risk of capture. If the real Robin Hood was actually running an organized gang of criminals rather than a shelter of the dispossessed and wronged, then we can be sure that they would be young men in their twenties. In Robin's day, everybody grew up fast – a child could be hanged for theft (the most common crime in any culture anywhere in the past) at the age of seven. Assuming he escaped the gallows, he would be an old man by forty-five.

Violence was a way of life in the Middle Ages. Today we have a daily press obsessed with knife crime, especially in London and a horror of how easily and cheaply knives can be obtained. In Robin's day, *every* male carried a knife, usually known as a whittle, and used it as much for attack and defence as they chipped pieces of wood. Women *never* ventured far from their homes or beyond a town's walls alone and wealthy men made sure they had armed retainers to travel with them on the roads. The monk in the ballad of the same name had a retinue of fifty. Although we do not have accurate figures for the population of the Isle of Wight in the fourteenth century, we do have statistics of murder. These were recorded in the coroner's court proceedings between July 1377 and Michelmas (autumn) 1392. Every single instance of it, over a fifteen year period, involved the use of a dagger. You were approximately two hundred times more likely to be stabbed to death in fourteenth century Brading than you are in London today.

Blood sports were hugely popular in Medieval England and with all classes. Bull-baiting with dogs, bear-baiting and cock-fighting (a game for children) were everyday events and drew large crowds, especially at fairs which proliferated in all major towns and many minor ones throughout the country. The boy who killed a chicken with a well-aimed stone took it home as a prize. Parents routinely beat their children and their animals. When Margaret Paston's daughter cut up rough about a man her parents wanted her to marry in the 1470s, both Margaret and her husband beat her around the head until she saw sense. Nobody, least of all Margaret's daughter, saw anything wrong with this. It was the same in the few schools that existed. 'Spare the rod and spoil the child' was a maxim that survived well into the twentieth century.

Against this background of danger, there was a need which has almost disappeared today, the need to belong. That meant there was safety in numbers. Lords had their retainers, who wore their livery and did their bidding, including fighting and killing. The barons' wars of the reigns of John and Henry III are examples of this, as are the fifteenth century Wars of the Roses. It is not accidental that the twentieth and twenty-first centuries have seen Shakespearean productions like *Macbeth* modernised into a gang war. Scottish and English politics in the Middle Ages was exactly that. Guilds formed to protect craftsmen and merchants from competition, driving out anyone who did not belong. Towns built thick walls with complex towers to keep outsiders out. And, in rather more unusual cases, we have men who sheltered in the greenwood or in otherwise inaccessible places to become outlaw bands.

The particular crimes with which Robin's band are associated are killing the king's deer and highway robbery. The Charter of the Forest, 1217, specified that poacher's dogs or horses should have their limbs cut off. Before that, at least in John's reign, the poacher himself lost both hands. Generally speaking, the part of the body that committed an offence received the punishment. So a poacher set traps with both hands. He fired a longbow in the same way. Exactly how a man was supposed to function without hands, assuming he could first get over the problems of shock, blood loss and sepsis, was not the concern of the authorities. In the case of the *king's* deer, such poaching was seen as an example of treason. Whereas heavy fines were the frequent punishment for non-royal animals, hunting the king's deer ran risk of the death penalty by hanging.

At best, though, killing royal deer merely provided poachers with venison for a limited time and, eventually, stocks would run out. To make a living, a man had to strike at travellers on the roads. With no satnav or even maps, long journeys by land were only undertaken in extreme cases. Most people lived and died in the parish where they were born and the highlight would be a weekly trek to a local town market or, height of excitement, an annual fair. For long journeys, asking the way was the only hope. In the 2005 movie *Kingdom of Heaven*, set at the time of the Third Crusade, someone asks where the Holy Land is. 'Go,' he is told, 'to where men speak Italian. Then go beyond, to where they don't.' It is a twenty-first century screenplay writer's joke, but it probably was not far from reality. In that situation, local landmarks, like the Major Oak in Sherwood, were indispensable guides. Most travellers went in numbers for safety, like the thirty-one pilgrims in Chaucer's *Canterbury Tales* or the fifty strong retinue that the monk has with him in the early ballads (see Chapter Two).

Great roads like Ermine Street and the Great North Road were the descendants of thoroughfares built by and for the Roman legions. They were straight where possible to enable troops to move quickly from one point to another. By the thirteenth century, all these had fallen into disrepair and they were patched locally, if at all, by amateur road-builders using substandard materials. Wheeled vehicles, of the type used by rich travellers, the natural target of outlaws, ran a constant risk of snapping axles or their horses throwing a shoe. And they were expensive, costing up to £1000 (almost £1million in today's money). There were probably only a handful of coaches in England in the early fourteenth century. Only women and the elderly used them. The wheels were six feet high and had no suspension, but there were painted and gilded interiors and heraldic exteriors and even gilded cages for pet birds. The cost of maintenance, of wood, leather, horses and their handlers, was prohibitive. Most people used simple country carts or wagons and these were used to carry freight like hay, flour or timber. By contrast there were ancient tracks everywhere – hidden lanes known only to locals and those were ideal for an outlaw gang to strike fast on the great roads and disappear again.

What do we know about outlaw gangs who feature in the historical record? Three things are noticeable about the three best known examples. One is that they were family 'businesses', pre-empting the Sicilian gangs of a much later century. A second is that the leading lights of those gangs were landowners of some status in their local communities, not the low-life we might expect. And the third is that they operated when central government was particularly weak and they could, literally, get away with murder. A very late example, and one unconnected with Robin Hood, is the Doone family, apparently Scottish exiles after the royalise rising by James Graham, the Marquis of Montrose in the 1640s. The Doones settled in the Badgworthy Valley, Exmoor and carried on a life of blackmail, cattle stealing and murder before they were wiped out by the authorities forty years later.

Another example is the Tuddenham-Heydon gang composed of two families of those names, who lived in Suffolk in the reign of Henry VI. Although these were in action two hundred years after Robin's time, their knightly status meant that they had money, land and armed retainers, not only to protect them against the authorities but to carry out attacks on strangers in the first place. In the 1450s, Henry VI was already an abject failure as a king. The son of the hero of Agincourt, he never came close to his father either as a ruler or general. Saintly, weak, charitable and artistic, Henry failed to control even his wife Margaret, who wore the breeches in the family and dictated policy. The whole period of the Wars of the Roses (1455-87) was one in which lawless bands of armed retainers roamed the countryside, bringing death and destruction much as the mercenaries called the Jacquerie had done in France in the previous century. This sort of brigandage had become a way of life and Henry was too unstable to do much about it. Both the term Jacquerie and brigand have their origins in the rough leather jacket (jack) known as brigandines which mercenaries of the period habitually wore.

Nearer to Robin's time however, was the depredation brought about by the Coterels and the Folvilles, dangerous families who fomented trouble exactly as gangland families have all over the world ever since. John Folville, who died in 1310, was Lord of the manors of Ashby Folville and Teigh in the neighbouring counties of Leicestershire and Rutland. He had seven sons, six of whom decided to break the law. Only the eldest, also John, inherited Ashby and remained law-abiding. His brother Eustace, who inherited the Teigh estate, joined forces with the Zouch brothers to attack a common enemy, Roger Bellers, baron of the Exchequer and right hand man of Edward II's favourite (one of several) Hugh Despenser. This brings us directly into Robin Hood territory. If 'comely king Edward' of the early ballads is Edward II, then we have a tangible link.

What we have here is typical gang behaviour, visible today in any major city or even small town. It is the stuff of the playground and some men (and even women) never get over it. Somewhere on the road between Leicester and Melton Mowbray, the Folvilles and Zouchs murdered Bellers on 19 January 1326. Once again, as with Henry VI, we are in the reign of a weak king. Edward II was also the son of a warlike sovereign, the 'hammer of the Scots', Edward Longshanks and once again, he failed to live up to expectations. Obsessed with handsome young men like Hugh Despenser and Piers Gaveston, he did what his grandfather Henry III had continually done and appointed foreign-born favourites over the heads of the native nobility (see Chapter Three).

Having hit such a high-profile target, the Folvilles and Zouchs took ship to safety; they had the money to do it. Politics changed direction quickly in Edward's reign and the formidable wife of the king, Isabella, turned on Despenser with the aid of her lover, Roger Mortimer and defeated him. The Folvilles were pardoned and came home, carrying out a series of robberies all over Lincolnshire, threatening, extorting and raping their way across the county. By 1328 there were four murders, three robberies and a rape laid at Eustace Folville's door, which are probably merely the tip of the iceberg.

Handily for the Folvilles. John, the only honest one, was made Keeper of the Peace in Leicestershire. This was a royal appointment which would in time become a magistracy, but family blood may well have been thicker than water and who knows how useful John was to his outlaw brothers? When another brother, Robert, turned on the others, almost certainly for money, he failed and was driven back in what amounted to a mini-battle. The king appointed Roger de Wensley to hunt down the Folvilles and the Coterels, operating in the same part of the county and when he caught them, he threw in his lot with them. The concept of a corrupt sheriff, nominally a royal official but in reality out to line his own pockets, comes out of men like de Wensley.

The situation with the Folvilles and Coterels is the same that probably applied to Robin Hood and certainly did to later American outlaws like Jesse James and the Youngers (see Chapter Eleven). They had friends, in high and low places, who would shelter them, lie for them and generally take their side against the law. The Folvilles had tenants and serfs on their estates on whose support they could count totally. They had protection, possibly for a time from the king; almost certainly from their upright brother. They even had the backing of the Church. In 1331, two monks, the cellarer of Haverholm Abbey and the canon of Sempringham Priory, paid the gang £20 to destroy the mill of a local rival. Two years later, they joined forces with other local family-oriented thugs, the Bradburns and the aptly-named Savages to kidnap Sir Richard Willoughby, one of the king's justices. They stole £100 from him and held him to ransom for the astonishing sum of 1300 marks (around £670,000 today).

The government had finally had enough and warrants for arrest were issued to over 200 followers of the families concerned. James Coterel and Roger Savage vanished into Derbyshire's High Peak Forest, where Little John is said to have been buried. Most of these men were never caught. Of those who were, most were acquitted by juries of their friends or strangers too intimidated to do otherwise.

The end of this story reads like a shoot-out in the Wild West. While Eustace appears to have had a change of heart, joined Edward III's Crecy campaign in 1346 and received a knighthood for his services, little brother Richard continued his lawless ways, nipping in and out of churches where he was able to claim sanctuary. Robert Colville (I too am suspicious of the similarity of this name!) finally caught up with them in one such church and, risking God's wrath, dragged them outside and beheaded them in the churchyard, one by one.

Robin Hood's merry men are, of course, a

very different collection of individuals. The later stories, enshrined in novels and movies, have them as married men, ordinary people in local, caring communities who have fallen foul of unjust laws based on property. Little John and Friar Tuck might crack heads with their quarter-staffs but they would not deliberately *murder* anyone. Their targets are always asking for it. They are greedy nobles, fat churchmen, dishonest merchants who have no concern for the suffering of the poor at all. Only in the early ballads does actual murder take place.

How, in a country with no police force, were such outlaws to be caught, even if the will was there to do it? The local community followed the Saxon/Norman system of frankpledge, that every male over the age of twelve had a duty to maintain the peace in the area. This was the Saxon notion of the tithing modified by the arrival of the Normans who introduced trial by combat to the existing method of trial by ordeal. The over-arching judge in both types was God Himself. The ordeal consisted of carrying a red-hot iron bar a specified number of paces. If the burns healed, a man was innocent. If they festered, he was guilty. In the case of combat, two men fought it out until one cried 'craven' or was killed. A loophole was brought in later in which combatants could appoint a professional champion to fight for them.

'I will be a lawful man,' ran the oath that every tithing man swore with his hand on a Bible, 'and bear loyalty to our Lord the king and his heirs, and to my Lord and his heirs, and I will be justiciable to my chief tithing man, so help me God and the saints.'

Like the oaths still used in law courts today, it

was a mantra and analysis of it uncovers some awkward realities. What if there was a dispute over a king's or a lord's heirs? Who should a man follow? What if the lord, or even the king, broke laws themselves (as they constantly did)? What could a man do about it?

The idea was that every man should look out for his neighbours' safety and well-being in a kind of neighbourhood watch among communities that were much smaller than ours today. Everybody knew everybody else and strangers were at once viewed with suspicion. This has never quite gone away. It is a fact, for example, that most instances of child sexual abuse are carried out by family and community members, not the semi-mythical wandering paedophile waiting for the opportunity to leap out at a passing child. Yet police forces and vigilantes alike today subscribe to the 'stranger danger' phenomenon with a naïve consistency. This is largely because 'such things don't happen around here' and everybody is convinced that their street, estate, village, town does not have criminals in it. Neither, of course, did Sherwood or Barnsdale!

The tithing men spoke up for an individual who was charged with a crime if they were asked to form a jury or to offer condemnatory evidence if any existed. In the event of a crime being discovered, everyone had the duty of joining the 'hue and cry', literally chasing a miscreant until he was caught. In theory, such a felon could evade capture by seeking the sanctuary of a church (all of which were kept unlocked) but as we have seen in the Folville case, that was no guarantee of safety. The ultimate example of the right of sanctuary being ignored comes from Henry II's reign. Having quarrelled with his bumptious ex-friend Thomas Becket, now Archbishop of Canterbury in 1170, the king may or may not (the jury is still out!) have sent four knights to kill him. They found Becket at prayer at one of his own altars in Canterbury cathedral and sliced off the top of his head.

The legal system was highly complicated, with the tithing at the bottom of it. From there, depending on the crime, certain cases were passed to the manor courts, presided over by a bailiff or reeve; or to the borough courts, where the mayor ran the show. Townships had their own courts, where the constable (one of the few Medieval legal terms to have survived) presided. Above that were the Hundred courts, a subdivision of the county, which had their own bailiffs and at the top (before the travelling king's justices took over for serious crimes) was the County court, where the enforcement officer was the shire reeve or sheriff. There were 39 of these in Medieval England.

The Church had a separate legal system of its own, which would have tried Friar Tuck had it ever come to that. It was precisely the issue of 'criminous clerks' (guilty clergy) that caused the rift between Henry II and Thomas Becket. Each insisted they be tried by their own lay or ecclesiastical courts. The problem was, whose law was being broken? God's? The king's? There was no easy solution. The 'cop out' clause for a man like Tuck, who could, if he and his exploits were real, be accused of aiding and abetting outlaws, was benefit of clergy. The bar was set ridiculously low. Any man who could read a passage from the Vulgate, the most common version of the Bible, was entitled to claim it. It meant exemption from the death penalty. So, if things had gone badly for Robin in his endless clashes with the sheriff, he and he Merry Men would have swung; Friar Tuck would not.

The sheriff was the king's man in local matters, the rough equivalent of the chief constable today and was kept very busy. On average, he would receive about 120 royal writs – the equivalent of policy directives from central government – and would have to act on them. If we have the impression that all the Sheriff of Nottingham had to do was to chase Robin Hood all day, the outlaw was either a far worse problem than anyone has realised or the writers of such stories had no idea what a sheriff actually did. That said, the sheriff had huge powers and few landowners would go against him. He had widespread powers of arrest and imprisonment, was not bound to act quickly to expedite trials and could legally order execution in certain cases. Oddly, the sheriff was not a judge – any more than today's policemen are – but most judges would be happy to go along with the sheriff's wishes.

The system was wide open to abuse and remained so for centuries. Nobody was above the law but few law enforcement officers were paid, so the pressure to take bribes was immense. Given that situation, it is easy to imagine that outlaw gangs became 'bands of brothers', dedicated to survival by any means; a classic 'them' and 'us' scenario.

What is more complicated is their communities' connivance in crime. Gangs like the Coterels and Folvilles, gangs like Robin's Merry Men if they existed, could only evade capture with the support of the people around them. There is no suggestion that the Folvilles even bothered to hide in a forest. They simply lived openly on their estates and raided at will. Anyone inclined to 'shop' them was silenced by intimidation or actual force. If we widen our net and look at other 'Robin Hoods', as in Chapter Eleven, we find a slavish adulation to them in some sections of society. Open any daily paper today and we find the same thing. A teenaged thug knifes somebody in a London street. There is no hue and cry. No one is dragged into the open and hanged (which was the Medieval concept of justice). Instead, the police usually meet a wall of silence or downright hostility. It was gang-related; the victim had been asking for it; it was drug related; that kind of thing doesn't happen in our neighbourhood etc etc. The same lame excuses are trotted out every time. And *if* someone is arrested, charged and faces trial – and none of this is a certainty – there will be dozens, sometimes hundreds of protestors who will back a murderer for a hundred and one reasons, almost certainly blaming central government (i.e. the sheriff of Nottingham) for 'creating' such criminals in the first place.

This explains why some criminals in the past – and Robin Hood is one of them – have been labelled 'loveable rogues'. Novelist Harrison Ainsworth caused far more trouble than he was worth when he wrote *Rookwood* in 1834 extolling the virtues of highway robbery in the eighteenth century. The actual robbers – Richard Turpin, John 'Swift Nick' Nevison, 'Sixteen String' Jack Rann, Jack Shepherd – were feckless ne'er-do-wells (in the case of Turpin, a dangerous psychotic) – but after Ainsworth's book, they were 'gentlemen of the road'. Turpin in legend rode his horse Black Bess between London and York in record time and to some, the only victim of his crime was Bess, who died carrying her beloved master to safety. Claude Duval would never rob a lady, but danced a minuet with her at the roadside, at the same time covering her male companions with a pistol! Readers believed this fiction, just as they believed the 'confessions' printed by unscrupulous hacks at the execution of a variety of nineteenth century felons. If Robin Hood was real and if he had been hanged for his crimes, outside Nottingham castle gate, perhaps, we can be sure that thousands would have turned out to see him turned off. And almost all of them would have been on his side.

CHAPTER FIVE

FRIAR TUCK – THE

CHURCH MILITANT

The Medieval Church dominated the lives of everyone, in all parts of Europe. It features heavily in the Robin Hood ballads, both via the curtal friar and a variety of abbots, who are usually wealthy and the natural enemies of the men of Sherwood. Priests were the only ones likely to be able to read and much of the news, especially of distant places, came via the pulpit. This gave the Church an extraordinary hold over laymen, but it also created a 'them' and 'us' situation. The priesthood could read and write, but they did it in

Latin (and occasionally Ancient Greek). While this made for cohesion among the clergy across Christendom, it meant that even the humble parish priest was an outsider in his own community. Remember how Sloth in Landland's *Piers Plowman* could not recite the Lord's Prayer 'as the priest syngeth' because it was literally in a foreign language.

At the top of the ecclesiastical hierarchy was the Pope (Papa) the spiritual father of his people who all claimed descent from Christ's disciple Peter, crucified upside down in Rome in 64AD on the way to that 'eternal city' becoming the headquarters of the Church. From the outset, the incumbents of Peter's chair continually disappointed. Early Church synods (councils of leading churchmen) met from time to time to discuss doctrine and liturgy. All priests had to be celibate. They had to take a vow of chastity alongside one of poverty and much of their time was taken up with charitable works. The obsessions of the early Christian church stayed with it for centuries. Even today, the insistence on celibacy causes more trouble than it is worth and much of the early synods' time was spent arguing over the date of Easter and the correct shape of the tonsure, the priests' haircut.

The Pope's domain was technically the whole of Christendom, the area where Christ was worshipped. His immediate see was the Papal States, an area which covered all of central Italy and which made the pope, like all other senior churchmen, a landowner on a massive scale. It also brought him into European politics from which there was no escape.

If we accept that Robin was an historical

character and that he lived in the 1190s, the two popes of that decade, chosen then as now from among the cardinals, were Alberto di Morra (Gregory VIII) and Paulo Scolari (Clement III). As was typical for centuries, these two were of noble Italian families. There has only ever been one English pope – Nicholas Breakspear, who took the papal name Hadrian IV in 1154.

A schism, one of many splits in the Catholic church hierarchy, led to rival popes being set up. One of these was Gregory VIII, often referred to as an anti-pope who was excommunicated (kicked out of the church) by the Council of Rheims. He lasted for a mere seven weeks in the top job! His successor Clement managed a more respectable four years. A third pope, Celestine III (Giacinto Bohoni) who took up the post in 1191, is remembered today largely for the *Liber Censuum*, a list of the Church's financial dealings and land holdings, reminding everybody who was in any doubt that the vow of poverty every churchman had taken had long ago been thrown out of the window, like one of Robin Hood's arrows.

If we believe that the real Robin lived in the 1260s, we find two French popes – Urban IV (Jacques Pantaleon) and Clement IV (Guy Foulques). Foulques had, as a legate – the pope's ambassador – been sent to England in 1263 to help Henry III in his war with the barons. Both these men espoused the causes of the French king in his on-going power struggle with the Holy Roman Emperor. Neither of them, incidentally, went anywhere near Rome itself.

If, on the other hand, Robin lived in the 1330s, then we have two more Frenchmen in the top job; Jacques Duése (John XXII) and Jacques

Fournier (Benedict XII). John was one of the antipopes at a time when the papacy (or at least one branch of it) had moved to Avignon in the south of France. The country was still sharply divided into its two languages of Langue d'Oel and Lange d'Oc; John needed a translator to read letters from the north.

And if the popes of Robin's day were Italian or French princelings, primarily concerned with the wealth and power of the papacy, what of the people below them? Popes were elected from among the cardinals who were originally priests of the various churches in Rome but by the twelfth century had become property-owning businessmen all over Europe, eager for promotion and power. Below them, and this is where the Church became regional, came the archbishops. There were two in England, the senior being the Archbishop of Canterbury and the junior, York.

Whenever we assume Robin lived, it is likely that York dominated. The first recorded archbishop was Egbert in the eighth century and his jurisdiction covered the whole of the north of England. He was one of the Lords spiritual who attended parliament on a regular basis in the thirteenth century and afterwards and his church was the astonishing York Minster, dedicated to St Peter and built on the site of an earlier church. Begun in 1230, its colossal towers, facades and Great Lectern make it a brilliant example of Perpendicular architecture. All bishops of York sign themselves Ebor, for Eboracum, the old Roman name for the city.

Below the two archbishops came the bishops and at this level we come into at least an element of the Robin Hood stories. The bishops of Lincoln and

Durham were both rich and powerful and represented the pinnacle of the Church's wealth and pomp as far as ordinary people were concerned. No popes visited England before the twentieth century and archbishops, by their numbers, were a rarity. The bishops however held services at their cathedrals regularly and took part in religious processions around their cities.

In Lincoln, the cathedral of the Blessed Virgin Mary was first built in 1074, but only the west front of that remains today. The current building dates from 1200 and, as is usual with cathedrals, took literally centuries to complete. The bell in the central tower is Great Tom which clanged out for miles over the surrounding countryside and one of the four existing copies of John's Magna Carta is on display today in the library.

In Durham, the present cathedral dates from the Norman period in the late eleventh century, including the central nave and the chapter house, where church administration was carried out. In keeping with all large religious foundations, Durham had relics of saints, those of St Cuthbert managing to survive two examples of Protestant iconoclasm, in the sixteenth and seventeenth centuries. As was common at the time, part of the cathedral was given over to a monastery. Today, County Durham is still referred to as the Land of the Prince Bishops.

It is here that the Medieval Church divided in its structure and purpose. Below the bishops were the secular clergy, the parish priests, men often surviving on a pittance in marked contrast to their lordly bishops, of whom there were seventeen in Robin's day. They too were celibate and often lived in their churches, small, wooden or stone buildings, scattered throughout towns and villages. As in any walk of life, the parish priests varied in terms of their abilities and morality, but by no means all of them subscribed to the letter of ecclesiastical law, especially on matters of poverty and chastity. When the church came under scrutiny with the rise of Protestantism in the sixteenth century, large numbers of the clergy were found to be illegally married, the fathers of children and often woefully ignorant. It is noticeable that the anti-Church element of the Robin Hood ballads dates not from an earlier, accepting period, but from the time when Henry VIII was breaking with Rome and dissolving the main source of Church wealth, the monasteries.

Aside from the direct route of the secular clergy from pope to parish priest, the monasteries and their sister organisations, the nunneries, were set up, in the words of St Augustine, to be 'civitate dei' (cities of God). These were populated by the regular clergy. It was acknowledged that the world was a wicked place, made so by the machinations of the devil who fought an endless battle with God for men's souls. Monasteries may be seen as an escape from all this, an avoidance of that confrontation, but, more positively, they were centres of piety where holy thoughts and deeds were paramount.

The very word monasticism comes from the Greek and means to live alone. Medieval monks were no longer isolated hermits, but their communities were deliberately built away from large settlements and by and large, they tried to be self-sufficient, growing their own food and fishing from their own rivers or ponds. The central figure in early monasticism was Benedict, horrified by the vices of his fellow students in Rome. He did indeed become a hermit to escape them and eventually set up a monastery at Monte Cassino in Italy, based on the tenets of work, prayer and reading. Manual labour was necessary, Benedict maintained, not merely to survive but because it created the healthy body that should accompany a healthy mind. The reading he had in that mind, of course, were the scriptures and a belief that every word of them was the gospel truth. Benedict's rule was tough. It included obedience to God that surpassed that due to the pope or king. Abstinence from the eating of flesh was important (hence monasteries' large fish stocks) and leaving a monastery could only happen in extreme circumstances. That said, considerable numbers of monks could be found on the road in the Middle Ages, which explains why Robin Hood meets so many of them travelling through the woodlands. They were on monastic business, which was considerable. The Church owned extensive property everywhere, often miles and counties away from the monastery itself.

The eleventh and twelfth centuries saw a revival of learning which has been called a renaissance before the better known one four hundred years later. Monasticism was part of this and between 1020 and 1120, eight new Orders were founded. These were the Benedictines themselves, called Black Monks because of the colour of their habit. The Cluniacs followed the same rules and began in the great French monastery at Cluny. The Cistercians were the White Monks, whose Benedictine rules were the strictest. They ate in silence and lived in grim cells with hard beds and no furniture, often wearing lice-infested hair shirts under their habits that ripped the skin. The

Carthusians came originally from the cathedral of Chartres.

There were also the Regular Canons – the Augustines and Premonstratensians, as well as the Gilbertines. These last were the only ones found in Medieval England, at Sempringham in Norfolk, where, unusually, monks and nuns were able to worship together in the same church.

The earliest missionaries in pagan England were Benedictines, two of them setting up the great monasteries of Jarrow and Canterbury. The distinction between a priory (run by a prior) and an abbey (presided over by an abbot) is simply one of size – abbeys are larger. When the monasteries were dissolved in England in the Henrician reformation of the 1530s, there were 200 such houses; at the height of Benedictine rule in the fourteenth century, there were perhaps 1,700 across Europe. The wealth of these houses was legendary. Both Glastonbury and Westminster were worth up to £3,000 a year by 1330 (£85 million today). Most of these religious houses had their equivalent nunneries, wearing the same coloured habit and following the same rules, presided over by an abbess or a prioress.

For both sexes, selection for life in monastic Orders was made early and usually by the children's parents. Traditionally, it was younger sons who had nothing to inherit from their fathers and plain girls who might never attract a husband (however sexist that may sound to modern ears) who were most likely to qualify for acceptance. Both sexes gave their souls and bodies to God, abandoning the idea of marriage or a physical, sexual relationship. How many of them remained true to those vows is impossible to say, but the idea of God's wrath was part of the indoctrination they underwent. True believers whipped themselves or were whipped by their brothers/sisters of the Order to atone for sins.

In the monasteries the day was divided into rigidly controlled time periods, punctuated by masses and prayers in Latin (sometimes Greek) over a twenty four hour period.

Early in the thirteenth century, St Francis of Assisi and St Dominic set up their own Orders which went in different directions. Dominic set up the Order of Preachers (Dominicans or Black Friars) which sent missionaries out into the world to combat the heresy of the Cathars in southern France who believed in two Gods – one good, the other evil. Francis, though associated today with animals, chose to follow Jesus through poverty, giving away his cloak to a thief who had stolen his hood. Both these men could be said to have created the friar, a new-priest-on-the-block in the thirteenth century which is where we find Robin's Tuck.

The friars came from the mendicant Orders; that is, unlike the Benedictines and their offshoots, they survived by begging. The Franciscans (Grey Friars or Friars Minor) were set up in 1209, the Carmelites (White Friars) the following year. The Dominicans followed in 1216 and the Augustinians in 1256. The oldest order was the crutched friars – so called because they wore crosses on their habits – in 1169. Which order Tuck belonged to is impossible to say, but if Robin did indeed exist and if he lived in the 1190s, Tuck had to be a Crutched Friar. Any later than that and his Order can only be guesswork.

By the middle of the fourteenth century there were 650 monasteries in England, with 200 Friaries

and 150 nunneries, adding up to over 1,000
religious houses. This represented a total of 20,000
men and 2,000 women. In addition to those, there
were hospitals (all religious foundations), private
chaplains, university lecturers (all churchmen) as
well as clerks to copy out Bibles and keep the vast
administration going. Overall, more than two per
cent of males in England worked in some capacity
for the Church.

One of the most realistic depictions of a
Medieval friar, albeit from a hundred years after
Robin's time, comes from Geoffrey Chaucer's
Canterbury Tales, written in the 1380s. We have to be
careful of Chaucer's account for two reasons. First,
the *Tales* are every bit as fictional as the ballads of
Robin Hood and second, the were written at a time
when the popularity of the Church was waning and
everybody, from the pope down to the humblest
priest, was just beginning to come under attack.
According to the Wife of Bath's tale, the friars were
everywhere, far more intrusive than sellers of the *Big
Issue* on street corners today. The official rules of
most Orders were that a friar's robes should be
made of 'vile and coarse' cloth, not the doeskin and
velvet habitually worn by abbots and priors. What
the friars did well in Chaucer's day and since their
inception, was to teach and they held impromptu
services/sermons in fields and high streets.
Traditionally, the cross outside St Paul's cathedral
was one such focus, but crosses and butter-markets
all over England would be guaranteed to have a
travelling friar hanging around them on most days
of the week.

The asceticism of, for instance, St Francis, was
lost on Chaucer's friar, who, like Tuck, has a

standard 'lay' name, Huberd. Francis had said that friars should be 'like pilgrims and strangers in this world, in poverty and meekness serving Almighty God', but Huberd, Chaucer tells us with his tongue firmly in his cheek, carries knives in his sleeves to sell to local housewives, either in exchange for money or for sex. He also knows the innkeepers throughout his area and he drinks like a fish. Even though this is fiction, it is likely that Chaucer was modelling his characters on people he actually knew or at least stereotypes that his audience would be familiar with.

Tuck falls squarely into this category. The curtal friar (the term may mean short-robed, but more likely is a corruption of Crutched) was one who operated from the gate of a friary and his roaming abroad in Sherwood or Barnsdale, wherever the Merry Men may have lived, is precisely what he was supposed to do. The roguish priest however could be merely a stock character in the Tudor May Day celebrations, introduced at a time when Henry VIII's dissolution of the monasteries was reducing the hold of the Catholic church on the people and actively driving them out of their communities. What better way to slacken this grip on society than to laugh at the Church?

In Robin's day, the Church called the shots. A man or woman was baptized into the Church: he or she married in the same church; they had their own children christened there; and when they died, they were buried inside the church if they were wealthy, outside if they were not. If you stand today in any Medieval churchyard, perhaps the one at Campsall, Yorkshire, where Robin and Marian are said to have been married (by Tuck?) or Hathersage, where legend has it Little John was buried (see Chapter Thirteen), you are standing on at least seven layers of people, each generation laid down on the one before and below it. And at the bottom, lies Robin Hood.

CHAPTER SIX

MARIAN: THE GOOD

WIFE

Maid Marian is almost an afterthought in the Robin Hood stories. She appears in none of the earliest ballads and may have been invented to become the May Queen to Robin's King in the Tudor festivities (see Chapter Eight).

Let us assume for the moment that Robin was real and that his light o' love was too. Marian's status would reflect his – it was most unusual for a woman to marry above or beneath herself. Although the Medieval period is long (about five centuries) and there are marked regional variations across Europe, generally speaking women in the Middle Ages were second-class citizens, demoted almost to chattel status at times. They were all, with very notable exceptions, pawns in what was almost exclusively a male game. We have noted already that the frumpish daughters of titled families often became nuns and traditionally, women who were past their best after a lifetime begetting children for their husbands, retired to nunneries as widows.

In the Roman law that held good in Europe and the Germanic tradition that filtered through to England as a result of the Saxon and Scandinavian invasions, attitudes to women were ambivalent. They are best expressed in looking at the two Marys of the New Testament. One was the Virgin Mary, married to Joseph, the Carpenter from Nazareth, who was singled out as a 'handmaid of the Lord' to give birth to God's son, Jesus Christ. As such, as portrayed in countless wall paintings, stained glass and statues all over Europe, Mary was untouchable. She represents purity, virginity and nobility in a way that no other woman could match. The other Mary is Mary Magdalene. She was healed of unclean spirits and spent the rest of her life devoting herself to serving Christ. Most interpretations see her as a born-again prostitute, a scarlet woman won over by God's love. This dichotomy, between the 'good' and the 'bad' Marys explain the mixed attitudes of most men.

But there was a third Biblical woman too and in many ways she epitomizes the views of most Medieval men. Eve was the weak one, the one seduced by the serpent Satan in the Garden of Eden, according to the Old Testament. She in turn seduced Adam, bringing down the wrath of God on the couple and condemning them thereafter. Snakes would lose their limbs and the power of speech. Men would have to toil in the fields in order to survive. And women would have to undergo the pain of childbirth. By the fifteenth century and in many examples before this, the Church condemned women out of hand because they were, above all, the daughters of Eve.

At best, Medieval women were seen as the weaker sex, physically and mentally. Excluding some remarkable women who *did* go to war in the Middle Ages, such as Eleanor of Aquitaine, the Lionheart's mother and, much later, Jeanne d'Arc of Domremy, women kept away from the battlefield except to tend, feed and clothe their men. Eleanor went on crusade with her first husband, Louis VII of France, and, according to legend, terrified the Saracens by revealing her breasts – and those of her ladies in waiting – to the enemy! Jeanne was altogether a more troubled soul, leading the French army of Charles VII against the English at Orleans. She was probably a figurehead only, not allowed to make political or military decisions. In terms of law, women were under the control of their fathers, before they came of age. The age of consent varied during the Middle Ages, but fourteen was considered an ideal age for marriage and its consummation. Since the purpose of marriage was procreation, the sooner a woman became fertile and conceived, the more children she could produce. Life, especially for the poor, was miserable and short; there was no time for protracted romances or long engagements.

Among the well-to-do, the nobility, gentry and

most of the middle class, if a woman's father died early, she would be taken under the wing of a guardian until she came of age. After her wedding of course, that guardian was her husband and even if she inherited lands and money, all a woman's worldly goods became her husband's on the wedding night. This remained the case until the late nineteenth century in Britain.

In practice, there are many instances of women holding their own in a world of men. Ladies ran their husband's landed estates, especially if said husband was away on crusade or, in the case of the Hundred Years War, fighting in France. Margaret Paston, a knight's wife from rural Norfolk in the fifteenth century, left letters in which she describes how their manor house can best be defended under attack and how many crossbows she should buy. The idea of the wilting female so beloved of the Victorian middle classes is largely a product of the surreal literature and music of the troubadours who sang about courtly love. The reality was very different. In the larger manors all over England, the steward or seneschal was the (male) officer in charge, but he usually acquiesced to the lady of the manor even in trivial matters like the day's menu.

The role of educating children fell almost entirely within a mother's remit. The father would be responsible, in a knightly household, for the military training of boys for the battlefield, but reading, writing, sewing and needlework (for girls), manners and etiquette, as well as religious issues, were the mother's responsibility.

Although at the highest level, women could not rule – the French, for example, introduced the Salic Law from the sixth century to exclude women

– there are other examples elsewhere of women doing just that. We have already cited Eleanor of Aquitaine, but Margaret of Denmark ruled that country as well as Norway and Sweden in the 1380s on behalf of her nephew Eric, then still a minor. The equally fierce Margaret of Anjou led her husband Henry VI of England's armies in the Wars of the Roses in the absence of his ability to do so.

The influence of women in Medieval culture was huge. In the twelfth and thirteenth centuries, titled ladies were the focus of the attention of troubadours and minnesangers, wandering minstrels who composed songs about courtly love. Marie de Champagne in France and Eleanor of Aquitaine in England were two just such sponsors. Courtly love was not altogether what the Church advocated. Married women could be the object of a knight's love as long as no physical contact took place and the yearning of a lost love was a powerful romantic notion in this artificial and rarefied world. In 1160, the French writer (we cannot call him a scholar) Andreas Capellanus wrote *De Arte Honeste Amandi* (The Art of Honest Love) which set out the manners and morals which defined courtly love. The rigid social classes which existed throughout Europe at the time were reflected in the amorous behaviour in Capellanus' work. Ladies became the centre of distant adoration, shown presiding over tournaments in Medieval tapestries and the knights who fought those tournaments – like the fictitious Ivanhoe – carried a lady's colours in strips of silk fastened to their armour.

Women were excluded from most walks of life except trade and there are surprisingly many examples of women running what today we would call businesses. Margaret Russell of Coventry once made £800 (a staggering £26m today) in one selling trip to Spain with her haberdashery. Within the Church, they were only allowed to become nuns, although the power wielded by an abbess or prioress could be considerable. Chaucer sneers at such women in *The Canterbury Tales*. His prioress, for example, speaks French with an East London accent. She spends a fortune feeding her lapdog titbits and wears a gold bracelet which Chaucer hints was given to her by a man; an inscription reads *Amor omnia vincit* (love overcomes all). At the highest level there are a large number of female saints in the Medieval world.

Marian's position is difficult to gauge because we cannot be sure of Robin's social status. In various recent movie plots, because he is a knight and former landowner, she has a similar status. She is occasionally called Marian Fitzwalter and is a royal ward, under the direct protection of Richard the Lionheart. In this context, she moves in the sheriff's circles and can play the spy on Robin's behalf.

If Robin was a villein – as opposed to a villain – that is, at the bottom of the social scale just above serf, then Marian's situation would have been very different. Villeins were bound by law and custom to their lord. She could no more choose a husband for love any more than a titled lady could (which perhaps explains the popularity of the nation of courtly love – it was a literary escape from forced and unhappy marriages). If her father let her marry outside the Lord's demesne, the father had to pay the Lord for the privilege, because he (the Lord) was effectively losing money as a result. If the woman were to become widowed, of which there was a high likelihood in the Middle Ages, she had to remarry within three months or the Lord would choose a husband for her. Refusal to marry would lead to fines and imprisonment.

The term 'Maid' is a confusing one for us. It does not imply someone in domestic service who works for somebody of a higher social status. It usually means a virgin or at least an unmarried woman. In that context, Marian is not Robin's wife but what today we would call girlfriend, jar though that word does with Medieval society. One thirteenth century writer reminded everybody that women were smaller, more demure, gentler and more delicate than men. They were also more loving and laughing, but likewise more malicious and envious. These attitudes would change as the centuries wore on, and not for the better. In 1484 when two monks were ordered by Pope Innocent VIII to draw up *Malleus Maleficarum* (The Hammer of the Witches) they accused woman of all kinds of evil. Even their long sleeves, which had holes cut into them, were 'the windows of Hell'.

Part of the problem about a woman like Marian's status in a male world lay in the Biblical attitudes we have already noted – Eve had demonstrably destroyed what would – should – have been paradise. The other part was the limited medical knowledge of the time. Doctors were few and expensive and their collective expertise amounted to a myopic faith in the third century physician Galen, with a smattering perhaps of Arabic ideas imported via the crusades. All this suggested that a woman's womb was cold (the four humours that Galen believed in were very susceptible to temperature) and only a man's seed could warm it up. Women then (as the authors of *Malleus* testified) were desperate for sex most of the time. It was a misogynistic idea which has survived to the present day and often leads to rather disappointing encounters!

Extreme though it is, and certainly never even hinted at in the Robin Hood stories, the crime of rape provided a Catch 22 situation in which women were *always* the victims. It was believed generally that an orgasm was necessary in women to conceive. If a rape was too brutal and there was no pregnancy, then a woman *could* accuse a man, but there would be no acceptable evidence (there were no forensics in a Medieval Court). If she *did* conceive, however, she must have had an orgasm and therefore, there was no rape. It was twisted logic, but it worked in favour of men every time.

Ironically, what worked against men may have been relevant to Marian and Robin. Had he been caught for theft and sentenced to death and if it could be proved that she was involved, all she had to do was to swear that she was operating under his orders/influence and she would walk! If all else failed and a marriage/relationship was a bad one, with the wife/girlfriend a victim of abuse, there was a special saint who could be prayed to – St Wylegeforte.

Despite the fact that Chaucer is cynical about his female church people, he has a more balanced view elsewhere – 'What is better than wisdom?' asks a character in one of his *Tales*. 'Woman,' comes the answer. 'And what is better than a woman?' 'Nothing.'

There is no suggestion in the Robin Hood stories of Marian being pregnant and giving birth, but in reality, it is highly likely that she would have done. There was no effective contraception – and even when there was, the Catholic Church frowned on it. Childbirth and pregnancy were huge risks in the Middle Ages. There were no forceps. Caesarean operations always ended in death for the mother. Ian Mortimer in *The Time Traveller's Guide to Medieval England* likens childbirth to 'Russian roulette played with a fifty-barrelled gun'. Nearly a quarter of women did not survive their pregnancies and it is estimated that over ten per cent of babies were stillborn. A further one in six would not make it past their first birthday, a statistic that actually worsened among the poor in the unbridled development of industrial cities in the nineteenth century.

Sadly, and once again, we are back in the hands of male writers and commentators; Marian is something of a cypher in the Robin Hood stories. The fact that she enters them so late, in the sixteenth century, means, as we have seen, that her character was probably shoe-horned in because there was a need to provide a May Queen to Robin's May King. Perhaps, too, it was an opportunity for relatively down-trodden women to escape for a few moments into a fantasy world of adventure and make believe. Only in the recent, largely screen-bound variations of Marion does she become a genuine heroine, capable of holding her own (see Chapter Twelve). As Ginger Rogers said, when asked whether Fred Astaire was the best dancer in the world, she replied that she was the better dancer, because she did everything he did, but backwards and in high heels!

Richard Denham

CHAPTER SEVEN

THE BOW

In all the Robin Hood stories – and some of the ballads – the one distinguishing weapon carried by the outlaw is the bow. For hand to hand combat, a sword was used, but a sword was a knightly weapon and the best ones, made in Toledo, Spain, were very expensive. The bow was traditionally a yeoman's weapon and as a war-winning tactic of the Hundred Years War (1337-1455) it was wielded by infantrymen before the use of artillery became safe and commonplace. The first recorded use of handguns was at Crecy in 1346, a spectacular English victory against the French but the first firearms were heavy, clumsy, slow to reload and could explode, killing their owners. Nine years earlier, Edward III had issued a royal proclamation that any other sport than archery for the common people was illegal, on pain of death. This had softened to imprisonment by 1363 but it was still frowned upon in official circles until the end of Elizabeth's reign in 1603.

The bow is an ancient weapon, used by the Egyptians, Greeks and Romans and just about every other army in the world. Mounted archers were never popular in England because, despite the Norman introduction of cavalry to the battlefield, the English style throughout the Middle Ages was to fight on foot. As a weapon of war and of the hunt, the bow was incredibly versatile and easy to use. The crossbow, which is also contemporary with Robin Hood, was far heavier and slower to reload, like the early firearms; and, despite recent movie variants (where the stuntmen are cheating), could not be fired with one hand like a pistol. The crossbow had to be loaded by placing a foot into the stirrup and pulling back the string onto a catch. A bolt or quarrel (arrow) with wooden flights was fired from it, the bow being held to the chin much like a rifle.

There is no doubt that the penetrative power of the crossbow was greater than the longbow. A bolt could pierce not just mail, but plate armour and because of this, the Church banned it for its barbarism. 'The crossbow,' wrote Anna Comnena, daughter of the emperor of Byzantium in 1148, 'is a weapon of the barbarians [by this she meant the crusaders of western Europe] … this instrument of war … fires weapons to an enormous distance … [the arrows] transfix a shield, cut through a heavy iron breastplate and resume their flight on the far

side, so irresistible and violent is the discharge …
Such is the crossbow, a truly diabolical machine.
The unfortunate man who is struck by it dies
without feeling the blow; however strong the impact,
he knows nothing of it.'

Interestingly, the Church's ban on these
diabolical weapons was only intended for Christian
versus Christian warfare; Muslims were fair game.

The longbow, by contrast, received no official
condemnation and it became the weapon of choice
for long-range warfare by the time of the Norman
conquest (1066). By Robin's time, bows were usually
made of yew, as the only English tree that provides a
genuinely flexible frame. A whole generation of
schoolboys, brought up on the Robin Hood
television series of the 1950s (see Chapter Twelve)
tried to make their own bows from other types of
wood and the results were pathetic. They also used
string and rubber-ended arrows, so the outcome was
anything but deadly! The yew was sometimes
reinforced with leather and horn and ultimately
bows were in a recurved shape, that is with the ends
of the bow facing in the opposite direction from the
firer.

The English longbow was six feet long (taller
than most of the men using it) and was developed
first in Wales. It probably gained acceptance in the
English army at the time of Edward I's wars against
the Welsh, in the early 1280s, at which point Welsh
levies using such bows were incorporated into the
king's service. Unlike the bows of the ancient world
– and probably this was still true of 1066 – which
were pulled back to the chest and were known as
shortbows, the longbow's string was pulled back to
the right ear before the archer let fly. Some

historians have doubted this, pointing out that evidence of the Bayeux tapestry which shows shortbows in use, is unreliable. True, it was made in the 1070s by nuns in England who had quite possibly never seen a bow in action on the battlefield; but the argument does not explain why the archers at Hastings achieved so little, whereas those of Crecy, Poitiers and Agincourt won those battles decisively. The answer *must* lie in a different kind of bow, a bigger, better one that achieved spectacular results. Arrows were 'a cloth yard' (three feet) long, iron-tipped and with goose-feather flights. Archers carried up to two dozen of these in quivers, leather cases fastened to their hips or at their backs and they practised regularly at targets called butts. This explains the number of places called Robin Hood's Butts dotted around the countryside (see Chapter Thirteen).

The longbow's range was up to 600 feet, although inevitably, its arrows did less damage at the end of that trajectory than at the beginning. The English longbowman's tactic, displayed brilliantly at Crecy, Poitiers (1356) and Agincourt (1415) was to fire en masse and rapidly. There was no time on a battlefield to pick individual targets and, unlike the movies where all sorts of protection is in place for animals, the enemy's horses were the better targets. They were larger than their riders and a downed horse would bring its own rider and probably several others down with it. There is, by the way, no truth in the nonsense that a plate-armoured knight, however he is brought down, could not get up again because of the weight of his armour. Such suits were superbly balanced and flexible, with hinged joints maximising movement. The average infantry soldier in the Falklands War (1980-2) was carrying heavier equipment than a Medieval knight.

Tradition says that the offensive 'V' sign originated in the Hundred Years War, when the French promised to cut off English bowmen's fingers. The 'Godamns' as the French called the English for their famous blasphemies, waved their bow fingers in the air to prove that they could still use them effectively. Arrows were removed from quivers and placed tip-down in the ground at an archer's feet. An experienced bowman could release between six and ten arrows a minute in a continuous stream of fire, designed to rain down from the skies in a deadly shower. Again, tradition has it that Harold Godwinson, the English king, was killed in this way at Hastings (actually Senlac) in October 1066 when an arrow hit him in the eye.

By the thirteenth century, the curved bow had notches cut into both ends to house the string which were made of horn and called nocks. In the absence of yew, not always available to armies on the march, ash, elm and witch-hazel were passable alternatives. In fact, by the time of the Hundred Years War, so much yew had been cut down in English forests that the timber had to be imported from Italy via Venice. The 'belly' or inside curve was made from the red heartwood of a branch and the 'back' or outside curve, from the sapwood on the branch's surface once the bark had been stripped.

Successive English kings after Edward III had insisted that all able-bodied men should own a bow and practise regularly. This continued well into the reign of Queen Elizabeth and statutes continued to be passed to prevent lads from kicking a football around when they should have been at the butts.

Edward IV had 14,000 archers under his command in the 1470s and the latest royal edict had warned against 'dyce, coytes [quoits], tennys … and many new ymagyned games', which were a distraction.

In peacetime, a lord often had a retinue of archers to help with the hunt; and hunting, for the aristocracy, amounted to an obsession. Although earlier examples are difficult to find, in 1467 the archers of Sir John Harwood's retinue received £10 a year (it had been only £1 a century earlier) and two gowns, and a house for their wives, as well as arrows and bows. The use of the bow, sadly, does not help identify Robin Hood's status. It was used by foot soldiers in battle, but aristocratic boys such as Richard Plantagenet, the future Richard III, were taught archery from the age of seven and provided with regular bowmasters to improve their technique.

Everybody feared English archers for obvious reasons – the speed and accuracy of their shots. A sixteenth century expert, having been brought up with stories of the Hundred Years War, wrote, 'The French turn up their tails and cry "Shoot, English!" … [and] the breech of such a varlet should have been nailed to his bum and another feathered in his bowels before he should have turned about to see who shot the first.'

Arrows were made from a variety of woods, but the favourite was aspen, then ash. There were at least four different heads – parallel-sided, barrelled (swelling in the middle) or the more usual tapered or chested (with the swelling towards the neck where it joined the shaft). The flights were 6-8 inches in length, bound to the shaft with spiral thread. Generally speaking, longbow arrows did less damage than crossbow bolts if they struck mail armour and rarely penetrated plate. Against a deer, of course, or an unarmoured man, they were devastating.

Today's experimental archaeologists have carried out extensive work on Medieval bows, even though they are cheating slightly. Before 1982, we only had one example of a genuine fourteenth century longbow. That was the year in which Henry VIII's flagship, the *Mary Rose*, sunk in the Solent in 1545, was raised and found to contain hundreds of Tudor weapons. These proved invaluable to researchers and are little different from the bows that Robin Hood would have known.

Modern archers, using careful replicas of these bows, routinely use draw-weights of 120-160lb, with a range of 360 yards (one fifth of a mile). Sir John Smythe wrote, at the time the Robin Hood ballads were gaining in popularity, that arrows used 'in the field [in battle] should reach 240 yards', but lighter bows (for hunting) could reach '24 scores' (480 yards). 380 yard ranges are recorded in Elizabethan butts. Barrage shooting has been duplicated by modern archers too. Clive Bartlett, using a 70lb bow, has fired 15 arrows a minute, all landing within a 12ft area at a range of 300 yards. If we take one retinue size that we know, Edward IV's 14,000 archers quoted above and even if each archer fired only six arrows a minute, that makes a hail of 84,000 arrows raining on an enemy in sixty seconds. Advancing archers could, of course, retrieve their arrows from the ground or bodies as they marched forward.

Each archer in military service was expected to bring a sheaf of arrows (24-30) and probably used two of these giving four to five minutes shooting time. If Robin really existed and if he fought at

Evesham under or against Simon de Montfort in 1265, we have no accurate information about archers on that day. The rebels were caught by Prince Edward's clever manoeuvring in a loop of the Avon, with deep, fast-flowing water on three sides and the royal army ahead. The usual tactic was for archers to open the proceedings before splitting their formation to allow the infantry to advance for hand-to-hand combat. The cavalry, usually formed on the wings or flanks of the main 'battle' would be sent in when it looked as though the rebels were wavering. It is interesting that many of the Welsh levies, who had virtually invented the longbow, deserted in droves before the battle began. This must have weakened de Montfort's archer formations.

The supply of bows for military purposes was vital. In 1359, three years after the English victory at Poitiers, 20,000 bows, 50,000 bowstrings (made, traditionally, of animal gut) and 850,000 arrows formed the arsenal at the Tower of London. The bow staves were made from carefully pollarded trees on special plantations, although Robin and his band would have used whatever was local to them. By the fifteenth century we even have a description of typical wood; the staves had to be 'three fingers thick and squared, seven feet long, to be well got up, polished and without knots'. In 1475, a bowyer (they had their own guild among the City of London livery companies) could make a single bow ready for use in less than two hours. The cost was 3s 4d (£152 today) making the whole thing rather less expensive than modern military firearms! In September 1465, just to taunt those of us trying to find the outlaw of Sherwood, one of Lord Howard's bowyers is listed as 'Robard Hoode'.

The tales of Robin's skill with a bow should be taken with more than a pinch of salt. They equate with the gunfighting stories of men like James Butler Hickock and Wyatt Earp. When we read eyewitness accounts of legendary gunfights like that at the OK Corral in Tombstone in October 1881, we realize that the two sides involved merely blasted away at each other for seconds and at very close range. Even then, several shots clearly missed their targets, which explains why most of the Earps and 'Doc' Holliday were still on their feet at the end of it.

The shooting contest described in the Child ballads (see Chapter Nine) relating to Adam Bell, Clim of the Clough and William of Cloudsely, although not written until perhaps 1505, is probably an accurate one (allowing for exaggerated skill) in use all over England much earlier. By referring to 'At such a but, syr … As men use in my countree', Cloudsely is implying that there are different types of archery targets rather as agricultural labourers, centuries later, had differently-patterned smocks, county by county. Cloudsely sets up two hazel sticks, twenty paces apart, and tells the king that he can split them in two. The king is dubious – '"Here is none suche", sayd the king, "Nor none that can so do".' Cloudsely, of course, proves him wrong. He then, in William Tell style, shoots an apple off his own son's head, and the king is so impressed that he gives him a job in the north as 'chefe rydere' protecting the royal forests.

'There's only one man in England can draw a bow like that,' was a phrase often used in the children's television series *Robin Hood* in the 1950s. The Kevin Costner movie *Prince of Thieves* and others, has Robin splitting an already perfectly placed arrow with one of his own (see Chapter Twelve. Not even the laws of physics can get in the way of Robin Hood's skill with a bow!

CHAPTER EIGHT

MAY DAY

R obin comes into his own as half fairy figure half human being in the May Day festivals which were the legacy of the Celtic Beltane. Life was hard for the average labourer in the Middle Ages and May Day was a chance to relax, drink and otherwise shrug off the miseries of winter. As authors Michael Baigent and Richard Leigh write in *The Temple and the Lodge* (1989), 'May Day would be, in fact, a day of orgy. Nine months later, it would produce, throughout the British Isles, its annual crop of children.'

The whole of spring was associated with rebirth and the Christian church cleverly stole the Beltane festival of the old Celtic religion and converted it into something else. Lenet was the

Saxon word for spring and in the Christian calendar, it became associated with the forty days in which Christ wandered in the wilderness. The Lenten fast was almost certainly a natural dearth when the food supplies ran low and Shrove Tuesday (pancake day) was celebrated with feasting before the enforced diet kicked in.

Likewise Easter, from Eostre, the Teutonic goddess of spring, became the allotted time to remember the crucifixion of Christ and to celebrate his resurrection. On Good Friday itself, country people would not use nails or iron tools because of the links with Calvary. The notion of 1 April, April Fools' Day, may have a connection with the god Lud, the prankster of the Celtic pantheon.

But all this was a build-up to May Day itself. Beltane was the official beginning of summer and the folk song 'Oh, it is the First of May, Oh, it is the First of May. Remember, lords and ladies, it is the First of May' has survived, possibly from Tudor times. The Celts lit vast bonfires in homage to the sun that they knew caused the much-needed crops to grow, but by the sixteenth century, this had changed and children and young people went into their local woods to collect greenery to decorate their homes, bringing nature to their hearths as symbolically as the harvest festival in September brought the products of the fields to be displayed on church altars.

The figure of Robin was introduced late to the May Day festivities but by the mid-sixteenth century it led to a complaint from Hugh Latimer, the Lutheran Bishop of Worcester, in a sermon delivered before the boy king Edward VI in April 1549. He was going home from London, when he found a locked church.

> 'I tarried there half an hour or more. At last, this key was found and one of the parish comes to me and says "Sir, this is a busy day with us, we cannot hear you; it is Robin Hood's day. The parish are gone abroad to gather for Robin Hood."'

Latimer was clearly furious – 'I was fain there to give place to Robin Hood.'

From what follows, it is likely that some of his audience found this funny –

> 'It is no laughing matter, my friends, it is a weeping matter, a heavy matter, under the pretence of gathering for Robin Hood, a traitor and a thief, to put out a preacher, to have his office less esteemed, to prefer Robin Hood before the ministration of God's word …'

The pompous bishop clearly had no sense of humour and his belief in Robin as a traitor and thief comes straight out of the establishment views held by the authorities of Robin's own time. Latimer's fierce Puritanism led to his death by burning under Mary Tudor six years later. Under the minority of Edward, the government fell completely under the Protestant/Puritan control of his regent, 'Protector' Somerset. When Edward died suddenly, probably of tuberculosis in July 1553, his elder sister Mary assumed the throne. Mary was the daughter of the Spanish princess Catherine of Aragon and immediately set about dismantling the Protestant church that had been building in power since the end of her father, Henry VIII's reign. Bishop Latimer was only one of several hundred victims of this religious coup.

The point about Latimer's rant is that he was aware that Spring celebrations and May Day in particular spoke more to the common man than the dry and cheerless scriptures that were his bread and butter. The Old Religion had survived the new. The Puritans detested Robin because he was associated with, at best, the Catholic faith and more probably, an earlier pagan past. Philip Stubbes, who today would be in psychiatric care, wrote his *Anatomie of Abuses* in 1583. He describes villages on Whit Sunday, man, woman, old, young, traipsing out to woods and groves, collecting branches and flowers to decorate their homes and themselves. 'For there is a great Lord present amongst them, as superintendent … over their pastimes and sports, namely Sathan, prince of hell. But their chiefest jewel they bring from there is their May-pole.' This was a huge tree drawn by twenty to forty oxen and 'this stinking idol' is adorned with flowers and herbs. Flags and handkerchiefs fluttered at the top and the villagers danced around it 'as the heathen people did'. Here was a man who believed every word of the Old Testament – dancing, music, happiness and Robin Hood had no place in that.

Stubbes' contemporary John Stow had a more balanced view.

'On May-day in the morning, every man would walk into the sweet meadows and green woods, there to rejoice their spirits with the beauty and savour of sweet flowers and with the harmony of birds, praising God in their kind.'

For two or three days, the festivities included Morris dancing and the consumption of a great deal of ale! Morris dancers supposedly arrived in England from Spain (the Moriscos were the Moors of Andalusia in the south of the peninsula) after the Black Prince's campaign at Najera in the late 1360s. Many of these groups still perform at folk festivals throughout the country, although the black-face tradition (in honour of the Moors of Spain) is now deemed racist by the new Puritans of political correctness. The music was generally of 2-4 or 4-4 time and the oldest surviving printed version is Arbeau's *Orchoegraphie* 1589. Among the characters taking part was Robin Hood, invariably dressed in green; Maid Marion, usually a man in drag; Friar Tuck as a clown and one or more hobby horses. There was a dragon, to terrify the crowd, with flames roaring from its mouth and Tom the Piper, he whose son stole a pig, according to the old children's rhyme. Such dances are still performed at Helston and Padstow and draw huge crowds.

In a society that was only marginally more prudish than ours (unless you were a Puritan) the Elizabethans saw May Day as a chance to let their hair down and, in fine old Celtic tradition, procreate. 'I have heard,' one commentator wrote, 'of ten maidens which went to fetch May and nine of them came home with child.'

Part of the festivities on May Day were the Robin Hood games, although it is not clear exactly what those were or when they were first played. The first record of them is at Exeter in 1426 and it may be that both Maid Marian and Friar Tuck were inventions to fit these games rather than linked to the historicity of Robin himself. Robin was the equivalent of the May King, with Marian as Queen.

On 16 April 1473, John Paston, the Suffolk knight whose letters are a fascinating social history of the time, wrote to his brother complaining about a servant who had left his employment 'to playe Seynt Jorge and Robyn Hod and the shryff off Nothyngham'. What Paston is referring to is the mummers' play (there are a number of varieties) which originally had no script and were a dumb show, relying on prat-falls, clownish behaviour and probably music. The these was always a fight between good and evil and gradually, in the sixteenth century, Robin replaced St George as the all-winning champion. Undoubtedly, the stories of the outlaw were already well known in rural areas where literacy was low and almost nobody would have read the printed versions of the ballads we looked at in Chapter Two.

Three years after the Paston letter referred to above, the parish clerk of Croscombe in Somerset recorded paying Richard Willis, presumably a local, to play 'Roben Hode'. In Wells in the same county twenty years later, a masque called 'tempus de Robynhode' was performed with a female dance troupe and much drinking. In the same decade, the churchwardens of St Lawrence in Reading were collecting money for 'the gaderyngs of Robyn Hod' – precisely the problem that so incensed Bishop Latimer fifty years later.

At Kingston on Thames between 1507 and 1529, regular expenditure was laid out for costumes, namely banner, coat, shoes and gloves for Robin, the Morris dancers, Friar Tuck, Maid Marian and Little John. What is interesting about all the examples above is that none of them took place in what we normally think of as Robin Hood's county, in other words, Yorkshire or Nottinghamshire. No doubt, pageants and May Day celebrations happened there too, but these examples show that by the sixteenth century, he was a national character, not just a local one.

As early as 1492, a group of men were summoned by the inquisitorial court of the Star Chamber in London to answer charges that they had dressed up as Robin and his Merry Men and behaved outrageously in public. Their defence was that this was a long-standing custom and the purpose was to raise money for their local church.

In 1500, Alexander Barclay wrote *Ship of Fools* and mentioned 'some merry fytte of Maid Marian or else of Robin Hood – but the characters were brought together' implying that the pair were not a couple but imported from two different sources for May Day purposes. In this context, Marian is not the demure virgin of later interpretations, nor the feisty female freedom fighter of the later films, but a loud-mouthed bawd on whom the Church would certainly have frowned.

Henry VIII took his Robin Hood games seriously. In 1510, when he was eighteen and had only been on the throne for less than a year, he crashed into his wife Catherine's chamber with eleven of his courtiers 'all appareled in short cotes of Kentish Kendal, with hodes on their hoddes and hosen of the the same, every one of them his bowe and arrows and a sworde and a buckler, like outlaws, or Robyn Hodes men.' Catherine's reaction, as a princess from Spain with no Robin tradition, is unrecorded!

Five years later, Henry was still hoping for a healthy son to succeed him. Catherine had gone through four pregnancies and lost all her children. In February 1515, she was delivered of a son but he died, like the others, shortly after birth. Perhaps it was to cheer her up that Henry arranged a treat on Shooter's Hill in what is today South London. Some two hundred of the king's own yeomen, dressed in green and led by Robin Hood, invited the royal couple to feast with them in 'the grene wood and to se how the outlawes lyve'. They dined on venison (the king's deer, of course) and then a masque was performed for them by ladies May and Flora, Humility, Pleasaunce, Vert, Vegetave and Sweet Odour.

By this time, Robin, Marian and Tuck had become subsumed into the Morris dancers and Robin had a dance of his own. What time was used and what specific steps are unknown, but in an odd way, this spirit lives on in the various Robin Hood pantomimes that are still produced in various theatres around the country at Christmas time.

Oddly, Robin became popular north of the border too. There have been various attempts to explain this, even tying Robin to the historical figure of William Wallace, who defeated Edward II's army at Falkirk and was immortalized by Mel Gibson in the movie *Braveheart* (1995). When Walter Scott wrote *Ivanhoe* in 1818/19 he was drawing on a character already known in the lowlands at least. Robin is first known in Edinburgh in 1492 and by the early sixteenth century had assumed a central role in the May games. He seems to have been a sort of master of ceremonies and judge, presiding over dancing, plays and a variety of games.

By 1555, either because of dour Presbyterian sensibilities or because of bad behaviour by the crowd,, the Scottish parliament banned any public displays involving Robin Hood or Little John. This obviously was only partially successful. In 1561, there were serious riots in Edinburgh when Robin festivities went ahead and the authorities stepped in.

By the end of Elizabeth's reign, Robin decreased in popularity and ceased to feature in the May Day celebrations. Whether this is linked with a similar decline in the national obsession with the longbow is difficult to say, but by the early seventeenth century, the King of the May was simply that, not Robin Hood specifically and Marian had become merely the Queen.

CHAPTER NINE

ROBIN'S RIVALS

The story of *Adam Bell* was first registered with the Stationer's department in 1557. In Tudor England, in what was very much a police state, all printed matter, including plays and poetry, had to be checked by the censors of the Stationer's office. This was presided over by the Master of the Revels, who was also responsible for the royal masques and other entertainment of the court. In the case of the *Adam Bell* poem, it seems that the story itself is much older, the earliest version dating from 1505 in the reign of Henry VII. Today, the usual printed version is the one collected by Harvard professor Francis Child in a collection of 305 such ballads, *English and Scottish Popular Ballads*, published in 1904. We shall look at Child's contribution to the Robin Hood legend in Chapter Ten.

The poem is extraordinarily long and in its original format may have been read – or even performed – to an appreciative audience. 170 'fyttes' or verses, mostly of four lines with an a,b,c,b rhyme, follow the unlikely story of Bell himself and his accomplices, Clim of the Clough and William of Cloudsely:

> 'Merry it was in grene forest,
> Amonge the leves grene,
> Where that men walke both east and west,
> With bowes and arrows keene.'

The greenwood, as usual, is the idyllic setting, but our three heroes have fallen foul of the law:

> 'They were outlawed for venison,
> These thre yeomen everchone;
> They swore then brethren upon a day,
> To Englysshe-wood for to gone.'

We have here the classic Robin Hood scenario – honest hunters driven to hide in the woodland for killing the king's deer.

'Englysshe-wood' is today Inglewood Forest between Carlisle and Penrith. Since this was originally a Celtic area later settled by Vikings and even Scots, the survival of an 'English' wood as a place-name is not surprising. For those who believe that Bell, Clough and Cloudsely were three of Robin's merry men, however, the geography is wrong – Carlisle becomes the new Nottingham, but it is nearly 200 miles to the north-west.

Adam Bell was very popular, reprinted at least seven times in the seventeenth century as literacy gradually spread. Bell and Clough are found elsewhere in sixteenth century literature, though not earlier. In 1575, Robert Dudley, the Earl of Leicester, held a lavish entertainment for the queen (almost certainly his lover at the time). Kenilworth castle, not far from Stratford where William Shakespeare was a grammar school boy of eleven, became the setting for several days of pageants, masques, music and merry-making, as part of one of Elizabeth's famous royal progresses. Robert Laneham, in effect Dudley's master of ceremonies, left a dazzling account of it all and mentions that Captain Cox from nearby Coventry, who, like Child three centuries later was a collector of songs and ballads, knew the rhymes of Adam Bell and Robin Hood.

Forty years after Kenilworth, Ben Jonson wrote his play *The Alchemist* which deals with various aspects of Jacobean criminality. In Act 1, he uses the phrase 'No cheating Clim o' the Cloughs', implying that his audience (essentially a London one) would be perfectly familiar with the rogue's name. Shakespeare also mentions this outlaw trio, this time Bell – '… hang me in a bottle, like a cat, and shoot at men, and – he that hits me, let him be clapp'd on the shoulder, and call'd Adam.' This was Benedick in *Much Ado About Nothing*, written between 1598 and 1599. Again, the use of Adam would have resonated with audiences and the name is used in the same way that Bishop Latimer used Robin Hood in his sermon in 1549 (see Chapter Eight) – as a generic term.

So what is the poem about? Three north

country yeomen (see Chapter Fourteen) form a loose brotherhood, all of them accused of deer-stealing. They hide in Inglewood Forest. While Bell and Clough are unmarried, Cloudsely has a wife and children and, not unnaturally, wants to see them. This means a trip to Carlisle. The town's history pre-dates the Roman invasion, but under the legions, it was an important military base called Luguvalium. By the fifth century, it was the centre of King Urien's kingdom of Rheged but fell to the endlessly marauding Scots in later centuries and did not become 'English' until the Normans took it in 1092, building a castle there in the following year. For centuries, the town was the target of the Border Reivers, outlaws without any of Robin Hood's charm and magnetism, who terrorized local areas with murder and mayhem. The Archbishop of Glasgow, Gavin Dunbar, put a colourful curse on them all in 1525. By the time *Adam Bell* was presented at the Stationer's Registry, the castle had been modified by the German engineer Stephan von Haschenberg to take gun-platforms and arrowhead bastions.

In the poem, whatever building state Carlisle was in at the time, Cloudsely visits his wife against the others' advice, but is betrayed by an old woman who has been living on his charity for the last seven years. With suitable ingratitude she immediately runs to the justice and the sheriff and turns him in. The fact that a justice of the peace is specifically mentioned implies that this story is set in the sixteenth century, not earlier, when justices had yet to come into their own.

The authorities effectively raise the hue and cry and a mob marches on Cloudsely's house which he and his wife, Alice, try to defend. The rest of the family escape out of the window using bedsheets and Cloudsely struggles on until the house is set alight and even his bowstring catches fire. He fights on but is overpowered and thrown into a dungeon, presumably in Carlisle castle, which served as a prison in the absence of a local gaol.

The gates of the town are locked and a gallows is set up for Cloudsely's hanging. But not everybody wants to see the archer swing and a boy sneaks out of the walls and gets a message to Clough and Bell. Using the subterfuge of what they claim to be a royal letter, the pair pose as royal messengers before strangling the gate-keeper and stealing his keys.

Cloudsely is tied to a cart in the marketplace awaiting execution by hanging and Bell shoots the sheriff while Clough hits the justice. This is enough for the mob, who run for their lives, their leaders badly wounded. The town mayor sends his guards to grab the miscreants but they fight their way out and get to their trysting tree in Inglewood. The tree – there are examples of this in the Robin Hood stories too – serves as a meeting place for outlaws. It is spelled 'trustee' and carried with it the notion of a safe house.

Alice has brought her children to the wood for safety and there is a happy reunion. Raising their archers' fingers to the authorities, they kill three deer and enjoy a banquet. Cloudsely decides to go to the king, to obtain what the poem calls 'a charter of peace', which approximates to a royal pardon. Thoughtfully depositing Alice with the younger boys at a local nunnery, the three set off for London with Cloudsely's eldest son. This again betrays the sixteenth century origin of the *Adam Bell* story because until the reign of Elizabeth, all monarchs were peripatetic, constantly on the move from castle to castle and palace to palace. No one could guarantee to find the king in London rather than anywhere else.

The king seems surprisingly reachable (there is no clue *which* king is involved) only guarded by a porter and usher. The porter in poems and plays of this period, like the drunken one in Shakespeare's *Macbeth*, was usually put in for light relief.

The trio kneel before the king and beg his forgiveness for killing his deer. He asks their names and they answer accordingly. Clearly the king has heard of their reputation (which by now involves several deaths among the garrison at Carlisle) and orders them to be hanged. If there are no fairy story elements thus far, there are now. The queen, taking pity on the three, reminds her husband that he has previously promised to grant the first boon she asks. Now, she is asking it – release the outlaws and spare their lives. The king agrees. It may be that this queenly intervention comes from the factual involvement of Philippa of Hainault in the reign of Edward III. Having taken Calais in the Hundred Years war, Edward intended to hang various burgesses from the town walls for having the temerity to hold out against him. His wife pleaded for their lives and the king cracked. He had done so earlier, in 1331 when tournament barriers in Cheapside, London, had collapsed and Edward was all for hanging the incompetent carpenters. Enter Philippa and all was well.

Timing, though, is everything and just as the king pardons the Inglewood three, messengers from the north arrive with news of the bloodbath caused by their escape from Carlisle. The body count is alarming – the sheriff and the justice have died of their wounds; so has the mayor, the entire peace-keeping force of constables and catchpoles and at least forty foresters, presumably town guards.

Bizarrely, rather than changing his mind and executing the felons, he takes them to the butts to see how good they are with their bows. Cloudsely splits hazel twigs at a vast distance and the king applauds him as the best archer he has ever seen. On something of a high, Cloudsely puts an apple on his eldest son's head and splits it in two at a distance of 180 yards. Had he failed, not only would the boy be dead, but all three outlaws would have hanged as a result. The story is that of William Tell, the Swiss archer (using a crossbow) who split the apple to thwart the evil machinations of Landberger Gessler, a minion of the Duke of Austria, in Switzerland in the fifteenth century. The first recorded mention of Tell, in a ballad and a supposed historical account, dates from 1470 so it is perfectly feasible that the anonymous author of *Adam Bell* had heard it somewhere.

The king, well and truly impressed by now, not only pardons the three but pays Cloudsely eighteen pence a day as a royal archer, with powers as 'chefe ridere' all over the north. Alice is made a royal nursemaid to the queen's children and the queen herself adds another 12 pence to Cloudsely's wages. The lucky boy under the apple becomes a wine-cellarer. There was a bizarre example of this outlaw-makes-good tale in the events of 1487 when a boy called Lambert Simnel (almost certainly not his real name) was put forward as the son of the murdered George, Duke of Clarence and therefore had a stronger claim to the throne than Henry VII, the Tudor king who had usurped the throne at Bosworth. Simnel's rising was put down at Stoke and Henry pardoned the boy, putting him to work at first in the royal kitchens, then as a falconer. Simnel died in 1525, loyal to the king to the last.

Similarly, the loyalty of the Inglewood three was never questioned. Content with the justice of their new lot, they go to Rome to be absolved of their sins by the Pope himself and die good men:

> 'Thus endeth the lyves of these good yemen,
> God sende them eternall blysse,
> And all that with hande-bowe shoteth,
> That of heaven thy may never mysse!'

The antiquarian Joseph Hunter tried to find Adam Bell and the others in the historical record, as we are trying to find Robin Hood. He believed he had found him and wrote:

> 'King Henry the Fourth, by letters enrolled in the Exchequer, in Trinity Term, in the seventh year of his reign and bearing the date the 14th day of April, granted to one Adam Bell an annuity of £4 10s [£81,000 today] issuing out of the fee-farm of Clipston, in the forest of Sherwood.'

Henry Bolingbroke, Duke of Lancaster had come to the throne by overthrowing God's anointed, Richard II and was duly crowned Henry IV. There were sound Medieval reasons for doing this, but the stigma of usurper never left Henry and he was troubled by it for the rest of his life. The seventh year of his reign was 1406 and in that year he was plagued with the rebellion of Owain Glyndwr who was trying to establish Welsh independence and he also put down a rebellion against him by northern lords who were aided and abetted by the Scots.

Hunter discovered that Adam Bell blew whatever little royal favour he had garnered by going over to the Scots (for reasons which are unclear) and forfeiting his Clipston estates to the sheriff of Nottingham. Hunter claimed that Adam Bell was an unusual name (it is not) and the Scottish link took the researcher to the border lands; in other words, not Sherwood, but Inglewood. The tendency to confuse Bell with Robin Hood was typical of antiquarian research where all sorts of folkloric nonsense was accepted with no critical analysis at all.

In fact the Bell family were well known around Carlisle and were as disreputable as the Folvilles and Coterels. They lived in Gilsland and Annandale, actively raiding farmsteads in the area and continually clashing with a rival family, the Grahams. Much of the Reiver criminality was clan-related and that translates in a sense into gang warfare. Christopher Bell was operating in Gilsland in the 1590s (clearly too late to be Adam the archer) and was guilty of theft, treachery and at least eleven murders. There was a price on his head. In 1616, Fergie Bell, known as 'the Crow' was wanted for theft. Thomas and James Bell were up to their necks in an all-out feud with the Armstrongs, claiming that the rival family had 'cleane rooted out' 500 Bells, beggaring 80 and kidnapping 60 more. Since there were less than 50 in the whole clan, this was pure nonsense; the Bells were liars for 'which God forgive them'.

Although the written record deals with the Bells much later than Adam's supposed existence and there is no reference to archery in any of their violence, it is at least likely that Adam was a Reiver himself. His stealing royal deer and killing royal officials chimes with a lawless family known to operate near Inglewood and Carlisle and the rest – Clim of the Clough, William Cloudsely and his family – were either invention for the sake of the ballad or were actual people whose names went unrecorded by history.

Just as well known as Adam Bell and his confederates were four men who could be counted as the rivals of Robin Hood. The first is Guy of Warwick, popular between the thirteenth and seventeenth centuries, who was the hero of several Romances on both sides of the English Channel. The Romances were not merely love stories, although that was an element of them, but adventures based on the theme of courtly love that we have mentioned elsewhere. Popular at first in the French court at Paris, the troubadours who sang those songs migrated to the English court, almost certainly via Eleanor of Aquitaine, the wife of Henry II and mother of kings Richard I and John. Guy is undeniably an English hero however and the usual plotline of the romances has him carrying out impossible tasks to prove his love for the beautiful Felice (Happiness). He kills giants like Colbrand, dragons, wild boars and a monstrous wild ox called the Dun Cow.

As with Robin Hood, it is not possible to date his first appearance in the written romances. The most commonly used today was printed in Paris in

1525, but there are older texts and it is not known whether Guy was a newly-created character (like Walter Scott's Ivanhoe three centuries later) or whether he is part of an older oral tradition of Medieval folk tales. The Victorians accepted Guy at face value. His sword was on display until recently in Warwick castle as was a rib of the Dun Cow. The animal was believed to have roamed the countryside near Dunchurch in Warwickshire, killing anybody that got in its way. Scientific analysis of the rib-bone has proved that it is actually a narwhal tusk and may have been brought back by Martin Frobisher, the Elizabethan explorer, on one of his voyages to what is today Canada in search of the elusive north-west passage.

Guy was believed to have gone on a pilgrimage to Jerusalem to atone for the violence of his early life and to have lived out his days as a hermit at what is today Guy's Cliffe outside Warwick. The Beauchamp family, who were earls of Warwick in the fourteenth century, built a chantry there and Richard Beauchamp christened his son Guy in 1298.

Is it possible to place Guy in the historical record? Emphatically not, but there are clues. It may be that the giant Colbrand was a Viking leader with the army of Sweyn Forkbeard or his son Cnut in their invasion of England in 1013. Likewise, the Dun Cow may not be an animal at all, but a variant of Dena Gau, the Danelaw. In other words, was Guy a Saxon warrior, probably not of theyn status or his name would have been written somewhere in the documents of the time. Although poems about Guy remained popular throughout the seventeenth century, we can be no more sure about his historicity than we can of Robin Hood's.

Bevis of Hampton is another rival of Robin, but he is far less of an Englishman than Guy of Warwick. Even though the Hampton referred to is Southampton on the south coast, Bevis's title is Count, which is not an English title at all. Nobility in this area were earls. The oldest written version, running to an astonishing 3,850 verses, is in Anglo-Norman and dates from the first half of the thirteenth century. There are similarities with Robin; Bevis has a loving wife, Josiane, and a loyal band of followers, not unlike the Merry Men. But there are more differences. Bevis, like Guy, kills dragons and giants (particularly the thirty foot tall Ascapart) and roves all over western Europe, travelling as far east as Egypt and Ethiopia. The use of disguise, imprisonment, escapes and fighting feature heavily in Bevis's romances, as they do in Robin's ballads.

The fact that Bevis's stories appear in Dutch, French and even Russian versions makes him difficult to pin down to any particular country. His stories, via Venice where he was known as Buovo d'Antona, were the first example of a non-religious work to be translated into Hebrew.

Hereward the Wake, unlike the last two contenders, is undeniably real, but while the stories of Robin Hood became popular as a result of the written ballads of the fifteenth and sixteenth centuries, Hereward disappeared largely from the public's perception until the novel *Hereward the Wake* was written by Charles Kingsley in 1865. Kingsley was a Christian Socialist vicar of the Church of England and his reformist books included the polemic on child chimney sweeps, *The Water Babies*.

He was also a misogynist and wife beater, but that was not generally known in his own lifetime. His *Hereward* underscored Scott's *Ivanhoe* in perpetuating the myth of the Norman yoke, that there was a visceral Saxon versus Norman feud which lasted for years after the Conquest.

Hereward (the Wake epithet means watchful, as in the quotation on Ripon town hall today – 'Unless the Lord keep the city, the Wakeman waketh in vain.') can be found in a number of contemporary sources. Unlike Robin, he was a landowner and that inevitably puts him in the historic record. He is mentioned in the Peterborough version of the *Ango-Saxon Chronicle*, the *Liber Eliensis* (book of Ely), the Domesday Book and especially the *Gesta Herewardi* (the deeds of Hereward). The *Gesta* copy is now in Latin but it may originally have been written in Old English.

Despite the fact that his parentage is unknown, Hereward was probably from Bowne in Lincolnshire and his family held lands in the area. According to the *Gesta*, which, like the stories of Robin, are prone to wild exaggeration and downright fantasy, he was a wild youth, being exiled by his father to the West Country and declared an outlaw by the king, Edward the Confessor. As a rebellious eighteen-year-old, Hereward fought as a mercenary for Baldwin V, Count of Flanders and married Turfida, from a wealthy St Omer family. He was still in exile when Edward died and the Normans invaded England.

By the time he returned in 1067, Hereward found his lands gone and his brother killed. The story begins to sound like Robin of Loxley in the later versions of the Hood legend. Frederick de

Warenne, whose brother William we know fought at Hastings under the Conqueror, threatened to kill Hereward, but Hereward beat him in a fight which most historians today accept is true. He then joined the army of Morcar, Earl of Northumbria, to take on the Conqueror himself. This was part of a general rising by troops who were not at Hastings in October 1066 and Hereward's other ally was the Danish king Sweyn Estrithson. Between them, they sacked Peterborough Abbey and took away its priceless relics. This may have been an act of sacrilege but Hereward saw it as a blow against the Normans who now governed every aspect of English life.

William himself came north to put the rebellion down, pinning Hereward in the isle of Ely, then a remote hill surrounded by marshland. The town was taken but Hereward escaped and his end remains unknown. There are theories that he was pardoned by the king or died in battle, possibly even going into a second exile from which he never returned.

The echoes of Robin are clear. Hereward is a man who has fallen foul of the law. He is an outlaw, driven to desperate measures by a cruel tyranny. If he *was* pardoned, then the circle of the later Robin stories is complete.

Fulk fitz Warwin is the least similar to Robin Hood but his historical record means that we can place him closest to the Nottinghamshire version of the outlaw. Je was born about 1160 and died in 1258 but most of the action in his life concerns the troubled reign of John. The Warwins almost certainly came over with the Conqueror but there is no mention of them as tenants-in-chief (barons) until the middle of the twelfth century. At that point, they held various Marcher castles, principally that at Whittington in Shropshire. The Marcher lands were important because they ran from Chester on the Dee to the Severn estuary, following the old line of Offa's Dyke, the Saxon earthworks built to keep the Welsh at bay. Castles here were crucial to the defence of the realm and it was vital that the families who owned them could be relied upon. For reasons now lost to time, John felt he could not rely on Fulk Warwin and for much of his reign was in a series of legal disputes with the Marcher lord over control of Whittington castle. Eventually, despite rebelling openly against the king in 1200-03, Warwin consolidated his lands and had the earlier outlawry overturned by Henry III in 1217. He went on to found Alberbury Priory in the 1220s which he gave to the Augustinian Canons. For much of the 1220s, he was defending his lands from the Welsh under Llewellyn the Great.

The ballad *Foulke le Fitz Waryn* dates from the fourteenth century and was written in a combination of English, French and Latin. By the time the Robin Hood stories were being printed in the sixteenth century, a new Middle English version of *Foulke* appeared on the market.

The rivals of Robin Hood did not command the attention given to the outlaw of Sherwood or Barnsdale. *Adam Bell* is so similar that it is difficult to see why it was written at all. Guy of Warwick was a hero too wide-ranging and cosmopolitan to be of much interest to the average Englishman, whose mind rarely wandered further than the boundaries of the parish in which he lived. Hereward and

Warin share the fact of outlawry with Robin, but their historical reality means that they cannot achieved, for example, the legendary feats of archery that the Sherwood/Barnsdale man manages. They are at once too prosaic and even ordinary by comparison with the greatest archer in England.

CHAPTER TEN

THE LEGEND GROWS

We saw in Chapter Two that the earliest ballads of Robin Hood were printed in the fifteenth century, a time when the printing press was revolutionizing the world. Printing itself was the creation of the Chinese, but it was unknown in Europe until this period. Before that, all books (and the Bible was by far the most popular) had to be hand-written, usually on parchment or vellum (calf skin). Traditionally, most Bibles were produced in monasteries, where the loving recreation of the scriptures was considered part of God's work.

The earliest printed books in Europe came from Germany, notably the Bible from Mainz in 1455 attributed to Gutenberg. Movable wooden blocks were replaced by metal and the complex Gothic script became increasingly the Arabic fonts that we know today. The earliest English printer was William Caxton, who learned his trade in Cologne and Bruges and set up his works near Westminster Abbey in 1476. His apprentice, Wynkyn de Worde, who took over the business after Caxton's death, was responsible for the best known copy of *A Gest of Robyn Hode*, illustrated with woodcut figures wearing the short doublets and brightly-coloured hose fashionable throughout Europe in the 1480s and '90s. There is no attempt at any historical accuracy.

The first of the later ballads, which, amazingly, did not appear in full until 1867, is *Robin Hood his Death*, which takes up where the *Gest* leaves off. Yet again, Robin refuses to die until he goes to 'merry Church Lees, My vaines for to let blood.' Most copies were printed in York (specifically Feasegate by Nicholas Nickson) and cost 4d in 1767. There are two versions of this ballad, which differ slightly, ending with Robin's slow death and his firing of an arrow through Kirklees Priory window to mark his grave. In one version, his epitaph is included:

> 'Robert Earl of Huntingdon
> Lies under this little stone.
> No archer was like him so good;
> His wildness nam'd him Robin Hood.
> Full thirteen years, and something more,
> These northern parts he vexed sore.
> Such outlaws as he and his men
> May England never know again.'

There is, of course, a negativity about the epitaph. On the one hand, it states without qualification that Robin was aristocratic (the rank of earl is second in the hierarchical table of the nobility) and on the other, he and his men are described as public enemies and the north of England is glad to be rid of them.

Robin Hood and Guy of Gisborne is undated, but probably stems from the late fifteenth or early sixteenth century. It is difficult to know what constitutes the early ballads from the later ones because they were not collected until the seventeenth century (see below) and not analysed until the late eighteenth century. The story is incomplete, with pieces clearly missing but what is important is that it introduces a character – Gisborne – who is rarely missing from the later stories. In Kevin Costner's 1991 movie *Prince of Thieves*, Gisborne is the cousin of the sheriff of Nottingham, neatly packaging the baddies together. What is even more striking about the *Gisborne* ballad is its violence, almost wholly missing from all other Robin rhymes; it is as though Ken Russell and Quentin Tarantino had collaborated in making a movie about the deeply disturbed and psychotic outlaw of Sherwood.

Most of the ballad deals with a duel between Robin and Gisborne, which Robin wins. Not content with killing the man, he cuts off his head and impales it on the end of his bow. We know that his was a ritualistic end for a number of people in the Middle Ages; Richard of York, for example, had his head placed on a spike over Micklegate Bar in York after he lost the battle of Towton in 1460. Even so, the usually honourable Robin does not come out very well in this story. He disguises himself as Gisborne and goes to Nottingham where the sheriff is expecting a triumphant Gisborne to return with the news that Robin is dead. The sheriff has Little John bound as a captive and Robin whips off his disguise and sets his lieutenant free. As the sheriff runs for his life, John lets loose an arrow and 'did cleave his heart in twain'.

From Nottingham in *Gisborne*, we move to Wakefield, where the *Jolly Pinder* lives. The term refers to the problem of stray animals in a society that had yet to enclose its fields. For eight centuries, the open-field of agriculture, brought in by the Saxons, was the only method of crop-farming. Animals other than pigs (which grazed the woodlands) were kept in meadows but without adequate fences or walls were constantly roaming the countryside – as sheep still do in parts of Wales, Scotland and the Yorkshire moors. The job of the pinder was to collect these wandering beasts – cattle were by far the most valuable – and keep them in the pound until ownership could be sorted out.

Probably dating from the middle of the sixteenth century, but not printed until the seventeenth, the *Pinder* is one of the increasing number of tough physical opponents who Robin cannot beat in hand-to-hand combat. So popular had the Pinder become that by 1599 he had a name – George-a-Green – and a play named after him. It is possible, given the 'green' connotation, that the character appeared in the Wakefield version of the May Day celebrations (see Chapter Eight). The ballad ends, as many of these later ones do, with Robin making the Pinder one of his Merry Men.

There are at least nine more ballads from the seventeenth century which follow the general style and strong line of what we have seen so far, but a couple stand out as being worthy of mention. *Robin Hood and the Curtal Friar* was easily the most popular from the 1660s onwards. The wandering priest who duels with Robin over the river crossing (an incident that features in virtually all the later versions) may or may not be Tuck (the name is not used) but he is generally assumed to be now. If so, then Tuck is a Cistercian from the abbey of Fountains in Yorkshire, which the ballad wrongly calls a nunnery. There *was* a Friar Tuke who was a real fifteenth century robber, but again, there is nothing to link him with the man who, in this ballad, becomes a member of the Merry Men. It is very likely that the Friar was a clownish buffoon seen in the Tudor May Day games (see Chapter Eight) and was shoe-horned into the legend along with Marian and Robin himself.

'Allen a Dale' first appears in a ballad as a harpist but he is more than a wandering minstrel. He loves a girl but she is taken from him by an old knight. The story dates from around 1600 but may be a nod in a much older direction – the Norman *droit de seigneur* in which a lord could take the virginity of any young woman in his demesne, whether she was betrothed or not. Unlike the usual combat tales, Robin here plays a match-maker, giving the girl away in church on her wedding day to Alan before making him one of his band (literally!).

These later ballads refer, in their explanations to tunes, usually established ones that listeners would know, and may imply that *all* the ballads were originally sung, at least in certain quarters. The explanation given to *Robin Hood and Maid Marian* is decidedly eighteenth century in flavour – 'declaring their love, life and liberty'. It was to be sung to the tune 'Robin Hood Reviv'd'.

We have seen already that Robin Hood became a stalwart of the May Day festivities so beloved of the Tudors. It is not surprising, then, in an age when the brilliance of drama should dominate, he makes an appearance on stage too.

Shakespeare mentions him directly in *As You Like It*:

> 'They say he is already in the forest of Arden and a many merry men with him; and there they live like the Robin Hood of England; they say many young gentlemen flock to him every day and fleet the time carelessly, as they did in the golden world.'

It is highly likely that Shakespeare had seen May Day performances, mummers' plays and masques, featuring Robin, so to link him with a romantic 'golden' past seems odd. Perhaps, even in the early sixteenth century, nostalgia was a buzz concept that playwrights could work with. The forest of Arden was never a serious contender for Robin's outlaw hideout, but it was well known to Shakespeare, just along the road from his native Stratford and features heavily in his *Midsummer Night's Dream* too. Robin also has a mention in *Two Gentlemen of Verona* – 'By the bare scalp of Robin Hood's fat friar, this fellow were a king for our wild faction!'

Shakespeare's career had not yet peaked when Anthony Munday wrote *The Downfall of Robert Earl of Huntington* and *The Death of Robert Earl of Huntington*.

These were written in 1589 and placed with the Stationer's Office (in effect the royal censor) in 1601. Munday was not remotely in Shakespeare's league. He was a London-born stationer (publisher), actor and polemicist who wrote anti-Jesuit tracts at a time when such men were believed to be Satan's agents and England was in the grip of Puritan fanaticism. He wrote eighteen plays and translated romances, mostly from French and Spanish and was anxious to end Robin's link with the May Day pageants:

'Me thinks I see no iestes [gests] of Robin Hoode,
No merry morices of Friar Tuck,
No pleasant skippings up and downe the wodde,
No hunting songs, no coursing of the Bucke.
Pray God this play of ours may have good lucke,
And the King's Majestie mislike it not.'

This was typical of a play's opening prologue, in which the actor speaking hopes for royal approval. The 'King's Majestie' in question was Henry VIII, in whose reign the 'play within a play' is set. Other playwrights, Ben Jonson, for example, found Munday's work decidedly average. The theatre impresario Philip Henslowe, who owned the Rose Theatre and bear-pits in Southwark wrote in his diary for February 1598 that he 'laid out unto antony monday' £5 for 'a play boocke called the firste parte of Robyne Hoode'. Henslowe was a notoriously tight-fisted payer but was used to dealing with theatre legends like Christopher Marlowe and

William Shakespeare and probably thought £5 more than enough!

It was Munday however who placed Robin once and for all in the reigns of Richard and John. He may have used the actual character of Fulk Fitz Warin (see Chapter 9) as Robin's basis and turned the yeoman-outlaw into Robert, Earl of Huntington, deprived of his title and lands by the vengeful John. Marian now becomes Matilda (a far more 'historical' name) Fitzwalter and it may be that Munday raided the anonymous *The Troublesome Reign of King John* for some of his material. It is possible too that he had read John Skelton's play, performed at Henry VIII's court in which Skelton himself may have played Tuck.

George Peel too found inspiration in Robin. Peel was the son of a London silversmith, attended Christ's Hospital and went up to Christ Church, Oxford. In 1591 his play *The Chronicle of Edward I* featured a Robin Hood game, in which Llewlleyn ap Gruffydd, the last Welsh prince, took part. The '90s was a busy decade for Robin. At the end of it, apart from Munday's work, he features in *George a Green, the Pinder [dog-catcher] of Wakefield* set in the reign of Edward IV from which the earliest ballads date.

In the next twenty years, Robert Jones wrote *A Musicall Dream,* a song collection and in some ways the forerunner of modern musicals. Michael Drayton, the poet laureate, included Robin in his *Poly-Olbion.* Richard Braithwaite mentions Robin's duels in *Strappado for the Divell* and *Barnabee's Journal.* Ben Jonson's own version was unfinished at the time of his death in 1637. *The Sad Shepherd or a Tale of Robin Hood* was full of supernatural imagery and its verse was not typical of the time or popular. Two and a half acts have survived and it was probably intended to be performed at the court of Charles I and Henrietta Maria.

Just as the plague closed theatres in London and other towns in the late Elizabethan periods, so did the Puritan-dominated Long Parliament in 1642. The Civil War had just begun and London was firmly in Parliament's hands throughout it. For over fifty years, the zealots inside the Church of England and those peculiar sects who deliberately left it, had railed against the Godlessness of the stage. Robin Hood, along with countless other legendary and fascinating characters, were put on hold as examples of 'Godlessness'.

With the Restoration of Charles II in 1660, the theatres re-opened. Those regicides who had signed his father's death warrant eleven years earlier were summarily executed or if dead – as in the case of Oliver Cromwell – dug up and dragged unceremoniously around the streets of London. *Robin Hood and his Crew of Souldiers* was put on on the day of the new king's coronation and is a fascinating example of an old legend adapted to fit the politics of the day, rather as twenty-first century celluloid Robins (see Chapter 12) must follow the bizarre precepts of political correctness.

The play was first performed in Nottingham, now firmly entrenched at the heart of the Robin Hood stories, which was, in 1661, a guilty town. Back in 1642, Charles I had raised his standard here against parliament and had expected absolute loyalty to the crown, as he did from all his towns. During Cromwell's Interregnum however, Nottingham had voted as their MP Colonel John Hutchinson, one of the Major-Generals of

Cromwell's police state and a regicide. *Crew of Souldiers* was Nottingham's way of saying sorry and pledging loyalty to Charles II. It tells us nothing at all about Robin Hood.

By the late seventeenth century, literacy was increasing to the extent that demand for books grew. There were broadsides, single sheets printed on one side only. There were garlands, which were collected autobiographies. And there were chapbooks, small, almost pocket-sized editions that were sold cheaply in marketplaces and fairs. Among later collections of these, printed between 1663 and 1670, there are no less than thirty-three Robin Hood stories and these, of course, are merely those that have survived by chance. Originally there would have been far more. Some of these were new; others were prose re-workings of the *Gest*. *Robin Hood' Golden Prize, Robin Hood and the Bishop, Robin Hood and the Prince of Aragon* all appeared in this period, along with many more. Interestingly, this was the time when the English national obsession with archery faded. By the reign of James I (1603-25) and certainly by the outbreak of the Civil War in 1642, no one practised with a bow any more, largely because firearms were now more reliable and effective.

The seventeenth century was also the time when Robin Hood place-names come into existence in abundance (see Chapter Thirteen) and proverbs entered the language. 'Overshooting Robin Hood' was synonymous with boasting; the long way round on a journey was 'by Robin Hood's mile'. A good business deal was 'Robin Hood's pennyworth' and so on. There was even one use of the hero as a simple epitaph to an unpopular landowner. When

Robert Cecil, the diminutive son of Elizabeth's chancellor, Lord Burghley, died in May 1612, his enemies chanted a rhyme about him in London, envisaging his gravestone inscription:

> 'here lies, thrown for the worms to eat,
> Little bossive [hunchbacked] Robin that was
so great.
> Not Robin Goodfellow or Robin Hood,
> But Robin th' encloser of Hatfield Wood.'

Enclosure, usually for sheep pasture, became the go-to tactic of progressive landowners in Tudor and Stuart England, but it was unpopular with the peasantry who resisted change. There is another link with Robin in Robert Cecil. As the Earl of Salisbury, he was secretary to James I and doubled as his spymaster. In 1605 when a group of Catholic conspirators were discovered plotting to blow up the Houses of Parliament, Cecil was watching carefully. On 9 November of that year, he wrote to Charles Cornwallis, the English ambassador in Spain:

> '… It is also thought fit that some martial men should presently repair down to those countries [counties] where Robin Hoods are assembled to encourage the good and terrifie the bad.'

It reads like the theme-song to the 1950s television *Robin* (see Chapter Twelve) but it also makes it clear that criminals and undesirables like the Gunpowder Plotters already had the generic 'Robin Hood' associated with them.

Where the later ballads were still in poetry form, they were sung, usually to existing folk tunes that everybody would know. *Robin Hood and the Tanner* was typical of the 'Hey down a down' ballads, so called after the second line of all of them. Where these were printed as broadsides, the quality of art was generally very average (as was the poetry) and, typically, reflect the artistic style of the time with no attempt at historicity.

Martin Parker's *A True Tale of Robin Hood* is fascinating for two reasons. Published in 1632, it not only purported to be an historical biography of the real man (whereas it was actually a ballad), but the artwork was lifted wholesale from William Thackeray's story of Adam Bell (see Chapter Nine). The frontispiece shows three armed men (originally Bell, Clim of the Clough and William Cloudsely) in full seventeenth century costume. Artists and writers alike had little concept of any time period other than their own, so we have glaring anachronisms; for example, in Shakespeare. Clocks strike in *Julius Caesar*, even though it would be fifteen centuries before they were invented. The Egyptian queen plays billiards in *Antony and Cleopatra*, a game unknown in the ancient world. So, although the three heroes in the frontispiece are armed with longbows, swords and halberds, they are also wearing the broad-brimmed plumed hats, doublets and Venetians of Stuart gentlemen.

'A True Tale of Robin Hood,' reads the top line, 'Or a brief touch of the life and death of that renowned outlaw Robert Earl of Huntington, vulgarly called Robin Hood, who lived and dyed in A.D. 1198, being the 9th year of the reign of King Richard the First, commonly called Richard Coeur de Lyon. Carefully collected out of the truest writers of our English chronicles. And published for the satisfaction of those who desire truth from falsehood.'

It goes without saying that there is no mention of Robin in any English chronicle and Parker's much vaunted promise to tell the truth is merely what today we might call fake news. It is intriguing, however, that, at the same time that Robin is portrayed in the chapbooks as a working class hero, he is elevated by the more discerning readers to the status of a earl and has definite dates attributed to an otherwise vague character from some time in the past.

The 1660s saw the arrival of what today is a vast industry in itself – the writing of 'true crime' books. Many of these today are badly written, spearheaded by a magazine outlet that relishes the gruesome aspect of murder, rape and sexual deviancy. In the decade of Charles II's restoration in England, William Winstanley wrote a 'Fanatick's Chronology', which covered dozens of villains from the world's first murderer, Cain of the Old Testament, up to the Regicides guilty of the murder of Charles I. The mad Roman emperors Caligula and Nero are there, as are Jack Cade, a rebel leader of the fifteenth century, Joan of Arc (every Englishman's femme fatale), Cesare Borgia and Copernicus, who never murdered anybody! Alongside these genuine historical characters are Tom Thumb, Guy of Warwick and of course, Robin Hood, Little John and Friar Tuck.

Robin appears too in the *Calendarium Astrologicum*, compiled by Thomas Trigge in 1665 and in Alexander Smith's 1714 *History of*

Highwaymen. Smith rubbished Parker's claim of Robin's aristocratic pedigree … 'for his birth was but very obscure … being no higher than from poor shepherds.' Born in Henry II's reign, Robin was, according to Smith, taught the butchery trade, but, being of a 'very licentious, wicked inclination' he took to highway robbery instead. There is nothing here of the hero. Before Harrison Ainsworth turned low-life into 'gentlemen of the road' (see Chapter Four), Smith dismisses Robin as a thug who had every opportunity to go straight and did not.

The eighteenth century saw, as we have noted above, the rise of the antiquarian, a collector of *anything* history-related and Robin got caught up in all of that. Thomas Percy, the Bishop of Dromore, Ireland, bought a manuscript from a Shropshire house and used it as the basis for his *Reliques of Ancient English Poetry* in 1765. This included *Robin Hood and Guy of Gisborne* which had generally disappeared from the market. Thirty years later, Joseph Ritson became the man who is probably responsible for the versions of Robin most of us think we know today. By the time Ritson was writing, Britain was at war with Revolutionary France, but, like other liberals of the time, Ritson espoused the revolutionary cause generally, supporting the traitor Tom Paine whose *Rights of Man* was a must-read for Radicals of his day. Accordingly, Ritson turned Robin Hood into a man much like himself, a rebel and champion of the people. He described the outlaw as 'a man who, in a barbarous age … displayed a spirit of freedom and independence which has endeared him to the common people … and in spite of the malicious endeavours of pitiful monks, by whom history was consecrated to the crimes and follies of titled ruffians and sainted idiots, to suppress all record of his patriotic exertions and virtuous acts, will render his name immortal.'

Ritson's Robin, like Martin Parker's, was born around 1160 and was probably of aristocratic lineage. He contends that his real surname was Fitzooth and that he died on 18 November 1247 – at which unlikely point the outlaw would have been 87! It is no accident that one of Ritson's friends was the novelist Walter Scott, who lifted Ritson's Robin almost wholesale for his Ivanhoe in 1818 (see Chapter Three).

There was a smattering of Robin-related books in the 1820s – Thomas Love Peacock's *Maid Marian* in 1822; Augustin Thierry's *Histoire de la conquête de l'Angleterre par les Normands* three years later. In both these works, the myth of long-lasting Saxon versus Norman enmity became enshrined, even though after 1070 there is no written record of any such attitude.

But another, in many ways more important, change took place before the middle of the nineteenth century; Robin Hood became a suitable character for children. There had never been a sexual element to the Robin stories and the rampant violence of, for example, *Guy of Gisborn*, was removed. A children's version of Ritson was produced in the 1830s and in 1840, *Robin Hood and Little John* was the first that specifically aimed at a young readership. Its author was Pierce Egan, best known for his sporting books on horse-racing, prize fights and cock-fighting. Robin, with his interminable archery contests, was not a million miles from all that. In this version, Robin is an aristocrat but raised by a woodsman, Gilbert Hood.

Across the Channel, Alexandre Dumas rewrote this slightly as *La Prince des Voleurs* (Prince of Thieves) in 1872. Robin, like Dumas' own musketeer heroes Aramis, Athos, Porthos and d'Artagnan, was a swordsman intensely loyal to his king. Across the Atlantic, Howard Pyle wrote a beautifully illustrated version for Charles Scribner's Sons, New York, in 1883. Robin's clash with Little John and with Friar Tuck are among the drawings that were copied and plagiarised countless times in the fifty years after publication.

The twentieth century *Robins* have largely been rehashes of the Ritson take on the outlaw as a social rebel. This was taken to be such a problem in 1950s Indiana that the state's Textbook Commission removed all Robin stories from their schools because the outlaw, stealing from the rich and giving to the poor, was clearly a crypto-Communist! It has taken the United States nearly seventy years to get over the 'Reds under the beds' of the McCarthy era.

The 1957 edition of the *Robin Hood Annual* is typical of the version produced for children. It cost 7/6d (around £9 today) and most of the illustrations are by G. Embleton, who cornered the market for accurate portrayals of weapons, armour and costumes of various historical periods. Robin is shown throughout as tall and handsome, usually laughing, with reddish blond hair and a goatee beard. His jacket is in Lincoln green, his shirt and hose red and he carries a broadsword as well as his trusty bow and arrows.

'Come to the Greenwood!' says the book's introduction, 'Robin Hood is calling you! And his band of merry men join in welcoming you to the green-dappled shades of Sherwood.'

It is clichéd and perhaps a little sexist by today's standards, but 1950s readers were not aware of any of that. 'Sturdy' Little John is there, so is 'dashing' Will Scarlett, 'jolly' Friar Tuck and (bizarrely and appearing nowhere else in the Robin stories) 'that super fighting man, Wat o' the Whip'. Needless to say, Tuck has not moved far from the fire, where a delicious stew, cooked by Marian, is bubbling in a cauldron.

The preamble sets the historical scene. England is suffering under the oppression of the Norman yoke – even though it is, by now, nearly 130 years since the Conquest – 'but in one Saxon heart the flame of freedom still burned with a fierce, unquenchable fire … one man had courage enough to defy and fight the ruthless tyrants … and that man was Robin Hood.'

Typical of the Annuals of the time, there are a series of stories, not unlike the original Rhymes, but with rather more cohesion and 'punch' (literally!) and the odd page of 'historical' information. The Major Oak is drawn and explained, so is Robin's grave and Little John's, as well as the modern statue on Robin Hood's Green near Nottingham castle gateway. There is also an account of another semi-legendary character, Hereward the Wake (see Chapter Nine), who challenged Norman authority soon after the Conquest in the marshlands around Ely, burning down Peterborough abbey in the process. The sports and pastimes page covers jousting, archery, wrestling, quarter staff work and hand to hand combat using sword and buckler, a small round leather shield.

If there is any doubt in the minds of social commentators as to whether young people read enough today, the disappearance of Robin Hood is living proof. As the poet John Keats wrote as early as 1818:

'Gone, the merry morris din;
Gone, the song of Gamelyn [a character in a later ballad]
Gone, the tough-belted outlaw
Idling in the "grene shawe";
All are gone away and past …'

Except that John Keats could not foresee the arrival of the cinema nearly a hundred years after his time. It is there that Robin Hood lives on.

CHAPTER ELEVEN

THE BOYS IN THE HOOD

Ll over the world a number of men have been described as Robin Hoods. They have much in common with the English original, all of them walking a fine line between national hero and common criminal. The fact that they lived centuries after the original Robin and thousands of miles away from Sherwood or Barnsdale, reinforces the fact that it is the universal qualities of the man in Lincoln green that have found a vast following of readers, listeners and viewers over the last four hundred years. What is common to them all is the comparatively late belief that they stole from the rich and gave to the poor.

EUROPE

There are any number of folk heroes across Europe, but they do not share the criminality associated with Robin Hood. Rodrigo Diaz, the Cid Campeador of eleventh century Castille, was an outlaw for a time in that he was exiled by his king, but no-one accused him of theft or highway robbery, despite a certain penchant for attacking fellow Christians as well as Muslim Moors. Similarly, William Tell, the crossbowman of Switzerland, lived as an outlaw (if we accept that he was historically real at all) because he fell foul of the Habsburg autocracy that ruled his homeland. Again, however, there is no record of theft or violence associated with him.

What is common to the examples listed below is that exceptional circumstances drove them to a life outside the law. That in turn made them heroes in some peoples' eyes.

The Hajduk (Sixteenth Century)

We begin, not with an individual, but with an ethnic and social group. The Hajduks were natives of various Balkan states who made a dubious living by serving as mercenaries in the armies of either the Austrian Habsburgs or the Ottoman Turks, clashing as both these states and regimes were over ownership of the same territory. Usually infantry, they were trained from childhood to fight and looked upon weapons as a means to an end. In the vicious religious wars of the sixteenth century, life was cheap.

It would be nearly 400 years before the Balkan states would win their independence and in the Hajduk era, the territory south of the Danube was newly won by the Ottomans bringing Islam ever further north. From that north, ever greater pressure was brought by the empire of Austria-Hungary, desperate to defend Christendom at all costs. For seasoned fighters like the Hajduks, this was a license to print money and some of that money, so the legend goes, was given by these free-booters to the peasant communities from which they came.

In essence, what we see in the Hajduks is an echo of the Saxon versus Norman struggle that forms the backdrop to the later English Robin – one band of men taking a stand against the dominating and usually unjust authority imposed on them from above. Although we recognize that this 'Norman yoke' was, at least in the long term, a fictional embellishment by later writers like Walter Scott, there is an element of truth in the Hajduk situation.

Kobus van der Schlossen (d. 1695)

The late seventeenth century was Holland's time. Emerging from the earlier oppression of Spain when the Low Countries were the Spanish Netherlands, by van der Schlossen's era, the country was united under its statholder and becoming extremely wealthy through exploration and foreign trade. The Dutch dominated North Sea fishing, especially of herring and would soon establish colonies in Africa and America. North Sea fishing in particular led to a clash with the ambitious sea-faring of Britain and a series of short, sharp wars were fought between them before 'Dutch William' was invited to become joint ruler of England with his wife Mary in 1688.

Van der Schlossen is a shadowy character about whom little is known. He served, as did many others in this section, in the army, which probably gave him a love of adventure, a sense of organization and a violent attitude which explained his criminal career. He deserted – desertion was all too common in seventeenth century armies – and formed a gang called the zwartmakers. They lived, à la Robin, in the forest of Slabroek, one of many huge European forests that make Sherwood and Barnsdale pale into insignificance. The gang's targets were wealthy local landowners and van der Schlossen earned a near-mythic reputation of being able to carry out miraculous escapes from various prisons. Finally captured at Uden, he met his match in the escape-proof and impregnable Ravenstein castle and was duly hanged there for theft in front of an estimated 20,000-strong crowd.

Juraj Janosik (1688-1713)

Another deserter, this time from the Habsburg army, Janosik is possibly unique in having killed nobody once he took to a life of crime. Legends of his generosity to the poor spread all over Poland and what later became Czechoslovakia. By 1710 he led a band of highwaymen who preyed on travellers on lonely roads in mountain passes where coaches could be stopped easily and there was a notable absence of help for the victims. The rudimentary police forces of the area confined their patrols largely to towns.

Janosik was finally caught in 1713 and was found guilty by a Habsburg court. His punishment was the usual one meted out for gang leaders; he was impaled on an iron hook and hoisted off the ground, bleeding to death in agony. In the last hundred years, there have been several novels and films with Janosik as a noble and much-wronged hero.

Schinderhannes (c. 1778-1803)

Johannes Bückler became a petty thief at sixteen in his home town of Miehlen in the Rhineland. It would be another century before Germany became a single nation and in Bückler's day, there were 300 separate states with different dialects, laws, customs and even religious affiliations. The boy was not content to stay on his side of the Rhine, however and found himself wanted by German and French authorities alike. His youth and good looks made him popular with ordinary people who almost certainly gave him shelter and support from time to time. He in turn doled out the horses and cattle he stole, transporting them across the river at night with the help of dodgy ferrymen.

At some point, Bückler joined the Austrian army (in that 'Germany' did not yet have one of its own) but he deserted and, like van der Schlossen, became a local hero because of his prison escapes. 40,000 people turned up to see their idol guillotined outside the gates of Mainz in 1803, the French method of execution believed to be the most humane in the world.

Bückler is today Germany's best known outlaw, the subject of dozens of plays, poems and novels.

Ustym Karmeliak (1787-1835)

'The Houdini of Podilia' was far more than just a legendary escape artist. He was born a serf in the Ukraine, an area which has been part of Russia on and off for centuries. Despite his humble origins – serfdom was in effect slavery and would not be abolished until 1861 – Karmeliak was literate in his native Ukrainian as well as Polish, Russian and Yiddish.

Serfs had no rights and as a teenager he was forced to join the Russian army where he served as a uhlan, a lancer. The Steppelands of his home were famous for their horsemen and it was in this capacity that Karmeliak fought Napoleon's Grande Armée in the notorious winter of 1812. In bitter and plummeting temperatures, men's hands froze to the locks of their guns and the cavalry killed their horses, slitting open their bodies to climb inside for warmth. Unsurprisingly, Karmeliak deserted (along with thousands of others) and set himself up as an outlaw attacking merchants on the road and labourers on their estates. The booty from this he gave to the poor, struggling serfs like himself. He was in and out of both the army and prison several times in the next few years and by the early 1830s had an estimated following of 20,000. He had carried out over 1,000 raids on country estates. We should be wary of statistics like this; the Russian government of the Tsars was notoriously lax and corrupt, especially in record-keeping, but if his 'gang' was even a quarter of this size, it made Karmeliak a rebel leader of some standing.

Supported by peasants and especially the Jews, he held out against the Tsarist agents chasing him until October 1835 when he was shot and killed, it was said, by a metal button, because he was immune to the lead shot fired by muskets. Karmeliak quickly became the focus of art, plays, poetry and folk songs throughout the Ukraine and beyond.

Tadas Blinda (1846-77)
Like the Ukraine, Lithuania was one of those states

on the fringes of Russia that would, in the twentieth century, become part of the Soviet Bloc. Blinda may well have been a political figure from the outset and the most likely thing to explain his turning to crime was that he had taken part in an anti-Russian rising in 1863. In Robin Hood style, he had a band of followers, who lived in the dense conifer forests near Byvaine.

For many years, Blinda's end was unknown but recently documents have come to light revealing that he was hanged as a common horse thief on 22 April 1877. The focus of plays, films and a television series, the first drama relating to him was called *Blinda, Leveller of the World*, at once giving him the political and social status attributed by later writers to the original Robin.

Rummi Juri (b. 1856)

The only Robin lookalike to be photographed from this European section, Juri Rummo (to give him his real name) looks every inch the surly criminal. Whether this is a studio portrait or a police mug-shot is unknown. He was born in another of those border Baltic states, Estonia, and made a reputation as a thief as well as a champion of the poor. There have been two films made about him, extolling his virtues as a folk hero.

THE EAST

The universal concept of a gallant thief with a heart of gold who is also a defender of the poor can be found in the eastern world too. No one we have met so far in this chapter was referred to as a Robin Hood because the possible existence of a Medieval Englishman of that name did not even extend to much of Europe. The same is even more true of Korea and Japan from which the next examples come.

Im Kkeokjeong (sixteenth century)

As far as the west was concerned, Japan, China and Korea were mythical, unknown places. Not until the thirteenth century would the travels of the Genoese explorer Marco Polo put them on the map, however incorrectly drawn. In fact, despite huge cultural differences between east and west, the same pattern of cruelty and corruption could be found everywhere. In Japan in particular, a master class of the ruling elite lorded it over downtrodden peasants and fought among themselves. In that sense, the politics was not dissimilar to twelfth and thirteenth century England.

Kkeokjeong was the son of a butcher from Yangju in the Gyeonggi Province of Korea. When the local warlord arbitrarily increased taxation, the peasants revolted and Kkeokjeong led them. Over the three years 1559 to 1562 he had hundreds of followers who killed the rich and provided food for the poor. His exploits did little to rock the ruling Josean dynasty who went on to rule for another four centuries however, but they did inspire a television series in 2008 called Hong Gil, which is the Korean version of John Doe. The whole thing may have been unhistorical (Robin Hood films always are – see Chapter Twelve) but it was proof of the fascination for us that such folk heroes still hold.

Ishikawa Goemon (1558-1594)

One of the most powerful of the sixteenth century Japanese warlords was Toyotomi Hideyoshi, who, while helping to unify a wartorn country, made enemies. Among them was Goemon, who attacked Samurai estates and redistributed wealth in the old-fashioned way. Whereas the English Robin Hood outwits and outfights his enemies, be they Guy of Gisburn or the Sheriff of Nottingham, Goemon's attempt to assassinate Hideyoshi failed. He and his son were boiled alive, the traditional Japanese method of execution for such crimes in 1594.

Goemon's spirit lives on however and he appears as the hero of countless Manga works, films, television series and video games. As we might expect from a Japanese hero, he has superlative ninja skills.

Nezumi Kozo (1797-1831)

Such was the cloying traditionalism of Japanese culture that the country Kozo knew would have been little different from that of Goemon two centuries earlier. It was still essentially Medieval, ruled by the Samurai code of bushido and its rulers tried as far as possible to ignore the west.

Kozo was born Nakamura Jirokichi – the nickname Nezumi Kozo translates roughly as 'rat boy', implying that he began his criminal career as a youthful pickpocket. In 1822, he was caught, tried, branded as a thief and banished from Edo, today's Tokyo. Undeterred, he carried on his criminal activities, this time as a burglar, targeting over 100 Samurai estates over fifteen years and amassing a fortune of 30,000 ryo (approximately £4million today).

By 1831, his one-man reign of terror was over and he was beheaded at Suzuganori, one of several official execution grounds in the Edo area. His head was impaled on a stake as a warning to passers-by. A tombstone marking his grave is still there, but it is not the original. Over the years, supporters have chipped away the stone as talismans, believing them holy. His charitable nature is largely unexplained, but since, when he was captured, he was broke, the assumption was made that he had long ago given the money away.

Inevitably, he is the hero of a Japanese television series.

Kayamkulam Kochunni (1818-1859)

Travancore was a princely state in the south-west of India which, in Kochunni's time retained its independence from the British. Ever since 1600, the French Compagnie des Indes and the British East India Company had been vying with each other for control of the lucrative Indian trade. Apart from each other, the main problem was the native princes, who had vast political power – and armies – at the head of a rigid caste system.

Exactly where Kochunni fitted into that system is not clear, but the fact that his family fell on hard times financially implies that he was not of the lowest lascar caste, the untouchables. The theme of a sudden, sharp reduction in circumstances is common to the later Robin Hood stories and dovetails nicely with the excuses given by criminals in courts of law for centuries. In true Robin style, Kochunni's targets were the rich and he gave generously to the poor. He died in Travancore gaol, most probably of one of the many diseases that decimated prison populations throughout India.

He did not become a folk hero until 1966, when director P.A. Thomas made a film about him.

Utuwankande Sura Saradiel (1832-64)

'The hero of Utuwan mountain' was an extremely handsome man (the only brigand in this eastern section to be photographed) and had the supernatural qualities of being both immune to bullets and invisible! He was born in Ceylon (now Sri Lanka) under British rule and took to highway robbery, targeting the rich and redistributing his loot among the poor. Arrested by the British police after someone informed on him, he escaped twice from prison and formed a gang in the Utuwan mountains, raiding from Kandy to Colombo.

Another tip-off in March 1864 led to his arrest and a shoot-out with the Ceylon Rifles. He was tried by an English-speaking jury in Kandy and sentenced to death. In keeping with a man imbued with supernatural powers, the rumours ran that Queen Victoria commuted his death sentence, but that a misplaced comma in her letter caused confusion to translators who interpreted it as a royal command to carry the execution out! Hanged and given a pauper's grave, he is today regarded as a freedom fighter rather than a thief.

THE WEST

In many ways, the existence of Robin Hood wannabees in the west is self-explanatory. The Americas and Australia were colonies of the British Empire and anything British, including folk heroes, was likely to cross the oceans as a result.

The Wild West in particular – western America in the nineteenth century – lent itself not only to a lawless breed of men who had little respect for morality and convention, but also to the rise of an adulatory press for whom no crime was too small to be reported.

Redmond O'Hanlon (died 1681)

The first example of a western Robin Hood is the nearest to home and before the advent of such a press. Ireland – John Bull's Other Island – had been a thorn in the side of the English for centuries. The Norman invasion of the twelfth century had set up the Pale, a narrow strip of territory policed by castle garrisons. Beyond the Pale (a phrase that has come to mean hopelessly uncivilized) were the native Catholic Irish, Gaelic-speaking peasants whose rural economy did not change for centuries.

James I had colonized the Irish north, Ulster, with Scottish Protestant landowners in the early seventeenth century but it was the English invasion by Oliver Cromwell, the Lord Protector, that created the crime spree of Redmond O'Hanlon. Destroying the towns of Wexford and Drogheda, Cromwell stripped local landowners of their property and the O'Hanlons were reduced to penury. Nevertheless, because of his aristocratic background, the soon-to-be-thief and extortionist was known as the Count.

Sounding rather like a gangster of the Capone era, O'Hanlon charged landlords protection money not to steal their cattle. He allowed his victims one chance to renege on their arrangement; after that, he killed them. He was a master of disguise, reversing his horse's shoes to confuse posses chasing him and wearing a reversible coat so that, at a distance at least, he looked like a Revenue Man. He became a champion of the downtrodden peasantry before his own stepbrother murdered him in County

Down in April 1681. In common with the tradition of the time, his impaled head was exhibited over the gates of Downpatrick gaol.

In legend, the Count lives on. There have been books, television documentaries and songs written about him and the County Down Gaelic Football Team are still called the Redmond O'Hanlons!

Joaquin Murietta (1829-53)

Since his death, Joaquin Murietta Carillo has been specifically referred to as 'the Robin Hood of the West', the first of our boys in the hood to receive that acclamation. California before the gold strike of 1849 was an inaccessible place, reached usually by sea rather than the difficult and dangerous route across country by wagon train. It was settled at first by the Spaniards, hence Murietta's name and the virtual elevation to sainthood of several of those outlaws.

Although details are hazy, it seems likely that Murietta was a Forty-Niner, one of thousands who flocked to the Californian gold fields in the hope of striking it rich. The story runs that he was driven out of his claim by greedy 'Anglos' who then proceeded to gang-rape his wife and lynch his brother on the grounds of horse-stealing (virtually a capital crime in the American West).

Out of revenge, Murietta targeted other miners, including 28 Chinese and 13 'Anglos', setting up a gang of four, all with the Christian name Joaquin! He was killed in a shootout with California State Rangers and his head put on public display. Posters at the time read 'Will be exhibited for one day only at the Stockton House, the head of the renowned bandit Joaquin! and the hand of three-fingered Jack.' Jack was another of Murietta's gang. There were doubts that the head was actually Joaquin's, but seventeen people, including a priest, swore that it was and there is no reason to doubt it.

Much of the giving to the poor (Mexicans) associated with Murietta comes from the 1854 Dime Novel written by John Rollin Ridge. It was a huge bestseller, translated into several languages and was one of the earliest potboilers being churned out by penny-a-liners for an increasingly literate public who could not get enough of lurid tall tales.

One of the last of these gave Murietta a new life. In *The Curse of Capistrano*, published in 1919, Johnston McCulley introduced a character called Zorro, a hero of Old Mexico, who leaves a fiery letter 'Z' with his sword-tip. He also wears a mask, the nineteenth century equivalent of the ubiquitous hood, an idea that would be repeated years later by the Lone Ranger on American and British television. There is little doubt that McCully consciously modelled Zorro on Murietta, imbuing him with an aristocratic hidalgo pedigree altogether missing from the man himself. Hollywood's silent movie industry was already underway and the rest is history.

Gauchito Gil (c. 1840-78)

Little Gaucho Gil was born Antonio Mamerto Gil Nunez to a farm labourer in Argentina. Working as a gaucho (cowboy) in the pampas, Gil somehow fell foul of the law, served in the Argentinian army, deserted and became an outlaw. He had miraculous powers of healing and of hypnosis and, like others in this chapter, was immune to bullets. He did his best to help the poor in the Robin tradition, but was murdered by the police, who dragged him into a wood and cut his throat.

Although the Catholic church refuses to grant him sanctity, he is still considered a folk saint in Argentina. His shrines, adorned with scarlet flags are everywhere and are regularly visited.

Chucho el Roto (1858-85)

Jesus Arriga was, like his namesake, a carpenter. 'Chucho' (meaning mutt) is a common variant of Jesus in the Hispanic world and 'Roto' translates as 'ragged'. Arriga was charming and able to cross socio-economic divides, especially where women were concerned. From the 1870s, he was targeting jewellery stores and the houses of the rich all over Mexico, using the newly-built railways to extend his theft zone and make fast getaways. Contemporary newspaper reports referred to him as Robin Hood and 'el bandido generoso' (the generous bandit). The authorities did not see it that way and he was interred in San Juan de Ulema prison in Mexico City where he died, probably of dysentery, in 1885. A number of plays and novels have been written about him.

Jesse James (1848-82)

'He is America's Robin Hood', wrote James D. Horan and Paul Sann in the *Pictorial History of the Wild West*. 'His yew bow is a Navy Colt; his jerkin is a faded blue coat. He never fails to distribute his stolen loot among weeping widows about to lose their homesteads.'

James came from a well-to-do family in Missouri, but the outbreak of the Civil War rocked the equilibrium of family life on the Missouri-Kansas border as it did in many areas. Whenever he was asked to explain his life of crime, James would say 'they drove us to it'. 'They' were the Union, a Federal government based in Washington DC which won an unconvincing victory over the rebel 'South' by April 1865.

James grew up riding with Quantrell's Raiders, thieves and cut-throats who used the war as an excuse to steal and plunder. With his brother Frank in tow and the Younger brothers as back-up, James turned to bank and train robbery as his speciality. The railways in particular reacted badly to this, posting huge rewards for James' capture in the hope that somebody would betray him. At first, the amount offered was $500 (itself a princely sum in the 1870s) but only a few years later, Jesse fetched an astonishing $25,000 (almost half a million dollar today) and Frank had to settle for $15,000 ($300,000).

The Pinkerton Detective Agency was brought in to stop the James-Younger crime spree, but got a bloody nose as a result, three of their agents being killed in a shoot-out in Missouri in March 1874. But the times were catching up with the desperados of the Old West. The Younger boys were blasted to pieces by outraged townsfolk in Northfield, Minnesota in September 1876 when they tried to rob the First National Bank; and Bob Ford had it in for Jesse.

Ford was James' cousin and had access to his house. On 3 April 1882, while Jesse was standing on a chair in his living room in St Joseph to straighten a picture, Ford shot him in the back of the head, killing him instantly. His tombstone reads, 'Jesse W.

James, Died April 3, 1882. Aged 34 years, six months, 28 days. Murdered by a coward whose name is not worthy to appear here.'

A number of films flowed from Hollywood, with superstars from Tyrone Power to Brad Pitt taking the title role.

Ned Kelly (1854-80)

If criminality is in the blood, Edward Kelly is a prime example of it. He was the eldest of three sons of an ex-convict. Between 1775 and 1837, Botany Bay was the official destination of thousands of convicts transported for crimes in Britain. The hard-luck stories are legion, but we should not impose our own standards of decency and compassion on the past. And even if a man or woman was not guilty to begin with, a life in the Bay created a disaffected class, unwilling to accept society's rules imposed from above.

In April 1878 the Kelly home near Greta, Victoria was raided by police on a charge of horse-stealing. By that time, Ned had already served three years for the same crime (in the United States at that time, he would almost certainly have been hanged) and he took to the outback, living on the land as a bushranger. The Kelly boys' gang grew and their reign of terror spread all over Victoria and New South Wales, cattle-rustling interspersed with arson.

They were finally captured in Jones's Hotel in Glenrowan and after a shoot-out with the police, during which Ned wore his now-famous armour made from ploughshares, the brothers were convicted in Melbourne and hanged in October 1880.

Kelly has not attracted the media attention of

many of the characters in this chapter. The film starring a miscast Mick Jagger was not well received.

Jesus Malverde (1870-1909)

Jesus Juarez Mazo is probably not real. Whereas all other potential Robin Hoods in this chapter have a basis in factual history, Malverde is probably a combination of two real outlaws, Heraclio Bernal and Felipe Bachomo, who were anti-government rebels in the same period.

The name Malverde comes from the fact that green (verde) is associated with evil (mal) in Mexico. What is astonishing about this man is not that someone so recent should be so shadowy, but that such a cult should have grown up around him. He is known today as the 'angel of the poor' and is particularly associated with drug-traffickers who regard him as their patron saint! Films have been made about him and he has lent his name to a whole raft of merchandise, including beer, oils and bath crystals.

What are we to make of the men in this chapter, who either contemporaneously or long after their time, have been associated with Robin Hood?

The inescapable truth is that some criminals, for a variety of complex sociological and psychological reasons, have a following in their own time and sometimes centuries later. They are 'lovable rogues' rather than dangerous sociopaths and most of us cannot tell the difference.

We believe, however, that the last words should come from Horan and Sann, whom we have quoted above:

'None of them was a Robin Hood. All of them spent their money for wine, women and song and there is no evidence that any of them gave a cent to a weeping widow or a helpless old man, despite the memoirs of senile old men, some of which have been accepted by historians.'

CHAPTER TWELVE

ROBIN AND THE SILVER

SCREEN

Inevitably, a transition was made between the stage and films. What had a dramatic appeal in Shakespeare's 'wooden O' at the Globe or Olivier's Old Vic, was revolutionized by the magic of the moving image. Robin Hood went along with it. Ever since the jerky, badly edited 'shorts' of the Lumiere brothers, William Friese-Green and other cinema pioneers, the experience of 'going to the pictures' captured generation upon generation. With its episodic ballad beginnings, a retelling of the

Robin Hood sagas lent itself to the studio sets, limited action and twenty-minute running time of the silent era. At least five Robin films were produced by American or British companies before the outbreak of the First World War, but it was Douglas Fairbanks' 1922 version that proved to be the first milestone.

There are conflicting views of when the first *Robin* was made. One version contends that *Robin Hood and his Merry Men* appeared in 1908; the other that it was 1912. Fairbanks' version ran, in one version, to an astonishing two hours, but we have to remember that early cinema-goers were mesmerized by the sheer magic of what they saw before them. The quality of acting, of screenplay writing (appearing as written cards between scenes), the costumes and the historical accuracy, were all secondary to the sheer experience of movement. Fairbanks was an acrobat, dancer and swordsman par excellence, with all the swagger we expect from a man who is prepared to take on evil Prince John and his dastardly accomplice, the sheriff of Nottingham. Fairbanks wrote the screenplay under an assumed name and his version of *Robin* was the first in Hollywood to have a gala, red-carpet premiere, at Sid Grauman's Egyptian Theater. Burly Alan Hale played equally burly Little John and would go on to do it twice more.

A history teacher reviewer of the movie on today's IMDb writes, 'Historically speaking, a mess … but sometimes you just have to say "who cares?"'

There were three or four *Robins* in the 1930s, with actors now having to project thanks to the new technology of sound, but the next milestone was *The Adventures of Robin Hood*, starring Errol Flynn, in

1938. For many, this is simply the finest *Robin* movie ever, Sherwood Forest never looking lovelier than it did in glorious Technicolor. In that sense, the Flynn version recaptured the idyllic setting of the early ballads, eternally summer and alive with the singing of birds.

As George MacDonald Fraser says in his *The Hollywood History of the World*, it does not matter who Robin *really* was – 'The legend is what counts and it was the legend that Warner Brothers brought to life.' Flynn had the same swagger as Fairbanks, but he looked far younger and brought a mixture of twinkling humour and stern determination to the part. 'You've come to Nottingham once too often,' says Basil Rathbone's Guy of Gisborne just before an epic sword-duel breaks out. 'Well, when this is over,' Flynn's Robin counters, 'I won't need to come again.' Flynn undoubtedly had the legs for tights but Rathbone was actually the better swordsman and movie trivia legend has it that the baddy had to hold back to let the goodie win.

Marian, played by Olivia de Havilland who was often Flynn's love interest on screen, was a gorgeous lady, lacking perhaps the feisty feminism of later versions. Again, trivia has a word about her horse; the beautiful palomino she rides through the greenwood (a colour and breed unknown in Medieval England) was Golden Cloud, a horse later bought by cowboy star Roy Rogers and renamed Trigger, 'the smartest horse in the West!' Alan Hale was Little John again, Eugene Pallette, huge and funny/threatening at the same time, was Friar Tuck. Apart from the creepily, dastardly Rathbone, Claude Rains was an oily Prince John, complete with immaculate fringe and a nice line in silks. His heroic brother Richard was played by tall, solid Ian Hunter. The dialogue was marvellous – 'We Saxons won't put up with this much longer, you know,' Robin warns the villains in his cut-glass Tasmanian/British accent. 'By St Ambrose,' laughs Tuck, 'a miracle!' As Fraser puts it, the movie was 'a reminder of the curious taste of the English-speaking people whose arch hero was a robber, a good loser and a kindly spirit.' The director was Michael Curtiz and the film won three Academy awards, including best sound track, a rollicking orchestral piece subsequently used in other Flynn movies.

Other Hollywood stars went on to play Robin but Cornel Wilde and John Derek could not come close to Flynn and nearly all later versions owed a great deal to the 1938 epic. In 1952, still basking in Technicolor, Walt Disney studios produced *The Story of Robin Hood and his Merrie Men* with a hardback book to accompany it. It trod the same storyline that they all do now – Robin defending the peasantry of the greenwood against Prince John and the sheriff – but this time, the hero was British. Ridiculously handsome Richard Todd was Robin, whose rolled-up sleeves look a little odd today. Todd was short as actors go, but this was the Fifties, when little Alan Ladd was holding his own against *much* bigger villains, so there were cinematic ways around all that! Peter Finch (actually an Australian) played the sheriff and by and large, the costumes were excellent.

There was a valiant attempt at authentic-sounding Medieval dialogue – 'what say you? Will you change your coats for mine? Twenty marks a man shall be your wage at Christmastide' – and if it is not totally accurate, it certainly makes more sense than anything out of the fifteenth century, as written in the early ballads!

The one irritating feature was Alan-a-Dale, the wandering minstrel who was constantly breaking into song. This was a feature of the less serious Westerns of the era too, at a time before the cowboy stars had a stark choice – go into Country and Western and on to Rock 'n' Roll or stay in the saddle. Even so, Alan was particularly annoying:

'O, I'll sing a song, a rollicky song,
As I roll along my way –
With a hey derry die 'n' a derry die do
And a riddle de diddle de day!'

Mercifully, scriptwriters do not write them like that any more!

Will Scarlett, spelt Scathelock in the book that accompanied the film, was suitably dressed in red. Because of the dyes involved, this colour was twice as much to make as green in thirteenth century Lincoln. The Merry Men's hideout is pure Disney – an unlikely (and very open) rock formation in the middle of the forest, which surely would have been known to *everyone*. Friar Tuck was played by James Hayter, surprisingly handy with a sword for a fat Franciscan. The scene where he carries Robin across the river is straight out of artist Howard Pyle's brilliant plates at the turn of the nineteenth/twentieth centuries.

This version is one of the few that features Eleanor of Aquitaine, Richard's and John's mother. The redoubtable queen, as Machiavellian and tough as any of her contemporary men, was played by the waspish Martita Hunt. Patrick Barr, complete with blonde/red wig and beard played Richard and the costume department even made sure he had a planta genista (broom) sewed to his surcoat as a reminder of his surname. Inevitably, the villains are defeated and Robin and Marian live happily ever after (were it not for the continued warblings of Alan-a-Dale!)

It was no doubt the success of the Disney film that led to Robin's first television outing in a six-episode series in 1953. Whereas today, television moguls are obsessed with endless repetition – episode after episode, series after series – long after interest and common sense has run out, in early television, programmes were often one-off or at best as a few episodes. This series, filmed and shown to British audiences in black and white, has not survived; there are no versions of it available today. It starred a future Dr Who, Patrick Troughton, who thus became the first television Robin in the world.

But it was the series that replaced that that marked yet another *Robin* milestone. *The Adventures of Robin Hood* ran from 1955 to 1960 and was shown as a half-hour black-and-white adventure slot for children, between five and six in the late afternoon/early evening. Whereas later children's television in Britain became hopelessly patronizing, repetitious and simplistic, the *Robin Hood* series, along with *William Tell, Sir Lancelot, Ivanhoe, The Count of Monte Christo* and *The Sword of Freedom*, brought historical scenarios to a growing and appreciative audience. It goes without saying that the generations who watched this version had little, if any, idea of an historical Robin Hood. They only knew of him from the annuals and other books produced in this era (see Chapter Ten). One critic today, remembering the series vividly, writes. It was 'not a children's program, not even a young people's program' because it was too articulate and thought-provoking for that. The series was written by two former Hollywood scriptwriters, both blacklisted under the ludicrous McCarthy witch-hunt which destroyed the careers (and sometimes lives) of socialist authors in America.

The star of this version was Richard Greene, an example of British 'beefcake' whose film career was almost over. *Robin* revitalised it and he became the quintessentially suave and gentlemanly Robin who could be trusted to handle any situation that comes his way. The first Marian (she was replaced halfway through the series by Patricia Driscoll) was Bernadette O'Farrell. A whole generation of schoolboys fell in love with her, but Richard Greene did not! The actors did not get on during production, so it was just as well that the producers insisted, because this *was* children's television, that there should be no scenes of intimacy. Archie Duncan played Little John; Alexander Gauge was Tuck. The sheriff was smooth, nasty Alan Wheatley, highly polished and dangerous. Audiences knew at once that he was the baddie, because he had a goatee, whereas Robin was, in the style of the '50s, clean-shaven.

The title song, by Dick James who went on to become the music publisher of John Lennon and Paul McCartney, is as memorable today as it was then. It opened with French horns ringing out across the greenwood, punctuated by Robin/Richard loosing a deadly arrow from his bow that thumped into an oak tree.

'He called the greatest archers to a tavern on the green,
They vowed to help the people of the king.
They handled all the trouble on the English country scene,
And still found plenty of time to sing –
Robin Hood, Robin Hood, riding through the glen,
Robin Hood, Robin Hood, with his band of men.
Feared by the bad, loved by the good,
Robin Hood, Robin Hood. Robin Hood.'

– which probably looks as bad as Alan-a-Dale's version above in cold print. But, as the '50s generation believed, but did not say, 'You had to be there!'

Disney returned to the Robin theme in 1973 with the first animated version of the story. Taking more than a leaf out of the studio's own *Jungle Book* of seven years earlier, a variety of animals played the key roles. Richard was of course a lion, bold and fearless. Prince John was a lion too, but scrawny and clearly the runt of Eleanor of Aquitaine's litter. Robin was a fox, underscoring the craftiness of an outlaw one step ahead of the sheriff's clutches. The critic Arthur Halliwell, always a difficult man to please, wrote, 'Alarmingly poor cartoon feature … especially dim and … quite lifeless.' Not even the voices of such illuminati as Peter Ustinov, Terry-Thomas and Andy Devine could give the thing much of a lift. A cartoon version is doomed to receive a mixed reception no matter what the subject. Purists object to the original being dumbed down and animation fans do not see the need for the original legend anyway.

Three years later emerged a movie which was completely at odds with the laughing hero of the greenwood. *Robin and Marian* had a distinguished British cast but its appeal was limited. Robin was Sean Connery, delivering his usual hard-bitten Scottish performance and Marian was Audrey Hepburn. The pair *looked* lovely, but this was the outlaw at the end of his life, after King Richard (Richard Harris) is killed at the siege of Châlus in April 1199. In a twist on the villainous prioress, it is Audrey who effectively murders Robin so that he can die in peace. Critic Geoff Brown wrote at the time, 'Surface realism only hides a core of mush suddenly revealed when the hero and heroine settle down for love-making in a field of corn.' On a practical note, the leads were only forty-six when the film was made, so rather young to be bidding the world goodbye, even in Medieval England!

Television restored the status quo in two mini-series between 1984 and 1986. Michael Praed was Robin, bringing an instant sex appeal that earned a huge teenaged girl following. He was replaced later by Jason Connery (whose father, of course, had already taken on the role) and the girls continued to scream. As one commentator told me, I gave Michael 8½ out of ten.; but Jason (like his dad) got ten!' What is fascinating about this version is the nod in the direction of the occult. Not only did the Irish folk group Clannad (Ciaran Brennan) produce the haunted *Hooded Man* soundtrack, but Robin was 'recruited' by the legendary Herne the Hunter, with his links to the supernatural greenwood going back to Celtic times (see Chapter One). Adam Bell, one of

Robin's rivals (see Chapter Nine) appears in one of the episodes, but the real innovation was Nasir the Saracen who becomes one of the Merry Men. This was an opportunity, at the dawn of the age of diversity, to introduce a black actor, but it set a precedent that has never gone away.

Nasir reappeared, this time as Azeem, in the next Hollywood epic in 1991. Azeem was played by that well-known Saracen, Morgan Freeman, who has one of the best lines in the film. 'What sort of name is that?' asks a blind man who obviously can't see Freeman's face. 'Irish?' Freeman looms over him and says, 'Moorish!' Kevin Costner was Robin and the title resurrected an earlier version, *Prince of Thieves*. The crusading element opens the film, with Costner and Freeman as prisoners of war. They return home to find that Costner's father (Brian Blessed) has been murdered by a cult led by the sheriff of Nottingham (Alan Rickman). Although the storyline is fairly conventional, there are some excellent variations. The sheriff has a pet witch (Geraldine McEwan) who can foretell the future and for obvious reasons, is afraid of Robin. Marian is the feisty Elizabeth Mastrantonio, strangely skilled in pseudo-Japanese martial arts as well as swordplay. Harold Innocent is a suitably slimy bishop, but it is Rickman who steals the show. Some of his lines were written by earthy comedian Ruby Wax, others were ad-libbed – 'and cancel Christmas', delivered as he is beating up one of his own guards – is a classic example. It was largely filmed in Malham, North Yorkshire, not far from the 'real' Robin's stamping ground and during the film, Friar Tuck can be heard humming *Bache Bene Venies*, which is an authentic thirteenth century song. Less authentic, but nonetheless top of the UK charts for sixteen weeks, was Bryan Adams' *Everything I Do*. There was even a Judas-like approach from Christian Slater as Will Scarlett, who does his best to betray Robin and the (uncredited) appearance of Sean Connery as the returning King Richard.

Two years later, Mel Brooks got his hands on Robin in *Men in Tights*. He had already produced a television series, *When Things Were Rotten* in the 1970s and that had its moments. Especially memorable was the *awful* theme song – 'Things were bad, and that ain't good. And then, came Robin Hood. Soon a Merry band he'd gotten … etc.' *Men in Tights* was a little disappointing. Rather like cartoon versions, you trivialise legends at your peril. The Saracen was now Asneez and Carey Elwes was suitably blond and bland as Robin. Arguably, the best thing in the movie was the tagline – 'The legend had it coming!'

Not until 2010 would there be another attempt at an historical Robin. This was the Russell Crowe/Cate Blanchett version, set squarely in the reign of John and, unaccountably, changing Hood's name to Longstride. Eleanor of Aquitaine, features, as does William Marshal, the redoubtable champion and adviser to her husband and both her sons, Richard and John. Otherwise, the movie failed. Oscar Isaacs made a suitably villainous John, but the French invasion scene, filmed from the air, shows what are clearly engine-powered amphibious vehicles hurtling towards the English coast (in 1216!). If Kevin Costner's Tuck got his music right, one of Crowe's characters did not. He is heard whistling *Frere Jacques* as a signal, even though the song was not written until 1775.

Robin Hood is a universal staple of screens large and small. There are currently thirty-five historical versions listed on IMDb, with a further seven in production. Three are Japanese Manga animations, no doubt with spectacular kendo swordplay and an astonishing fifty-eight more have the name Robin Hood in the title, but lack the actual character or the Medieval setting. Recent productions have largely sunk without trace, mixing modern costumes, futuristic concepts and of course, political correctness in an attempt to catch audiences' endless appetites for box sets. No doubt, some of these will have an appeal. One reviewer of the 1969 *Erotic Adventures of Robin Hood* wrote that the storyline is preferable to either the Costner or Crowe versions. *The Ghosts of Sherwood* in 2012 was in effect a zombie movie and the *Robin Hood* of 2017 had, predictably, a female Robin. It has no reviews at all on IMDb.

CHAPTER THIRTEEN

THE PLACES OF ROBIN

As we have seen, there are three possible historical Robin Hoods; one in the reign of Richard the Lionheart, the other rather later, in the reign of Edward I and a third in the reign of Edward II. Can we pin this down by looking at the places around the country associated with him?

Discounting the hundreds of pubs and streets that have hijacked his name for no reason at all – one example is that of the street and pub in Pan, Newport, Isle of Wight, which has no possible link with the man or the legend – there are, according to one website, 159 relevant place names in England. There is even one in Wales. Of the 159, sixteen are in Nottinghamshire, seven in Derbyshire and twenty-four in Yorkshire; the rest are scattered. This would tend to suggest, though it is by no means a certainty, that Yorkshire is the likely focus of the stories; Robin Hood was a Yorkshireman. By contrast, Little John has only ten place names and poor old Friar Tuck only one.

Place names are notoriously difficult and confusing. Hood, for instance, has sometimes been taken as a variant of Odin, the Norse god and the several spellings of the outlaw's surname do not help. Bearing in mind that both Nottingham, with its Sherwood Forest links and Yorkshire were in the north-east of England in that area known as the Danelaw, the confusion with Norse mythology becomes even greater.

Any number of place types are associated with Robin. He is the owner of lanes, graves, cottages, hills, farms, granges, crofts, towers, crosses, fields, butts, acres, stables, larders, seats, whetstones, meadows, wells, parks, beds, strides, tumps, tables, bridges, rows, bowers, walks, courts, yards, bogs, islands and balls. In a unique instance, he is linked with pricking rods (Megalithic stone pillars).

The five Robin Hood sites in Richmond Park, Surrey, can easily be linked with Henry VIII who seems to have had an affinity with the figure of Robin via the May Day festivities of which the Tudor king was so fond (see Chapter Eight).

Today, most people associate Robin with Sherwood and Nottingham, so we will begin there.

Sherwood Forest

We know that Medieval England was heavily forested, although this has been exaggerated. Some areas of Sherwood were probably impenetrable but others were open heathland by the time of the Norman Conquest and hardly suitable hiding places for a desperate band of cut-throats. Pollen sampling surveys recently carried out prove that Sherwood existed by the end of the Ice Age and today it covers a relatively small 1,045 acres. In the twelfth and thirteenth centuries, it was perhaps four times that size, a royal hunting forest teeming with game, especially deer.

In the centre stood Thynghowe, an important meeting place under the local government in the Danelaw. Thyng roughly translates to a council or parliament and is mentioned as still in existence in documents dating to 1334. The area was rediscovered by the work of local historians in 2005-6.

The oldest tree in the Forest is the Major Oak, with such a vast trunk that legend has it that all the Merry Men could hide inside it. Dendrochronology has dated the tree to between 800 and 1,000 years old, so it would probably not have been particularly large in Robin Hood's day. From Victorian times, the Oak has been supported with scaffolding. Nearby is the Centre Tree, a marker from which Robin's secret paths radiated in all directions.

All that can be said of Sherwood is that it *could* have been the home to an outlaw gang. It is near enough to local towns for the Merry Men to obtain goods they could not otherwise have obtained and near enough to the Great North Road between York and London to rob wealthy travellers.

Nottingham

In pre-Roman times, the town was Tig Guocobauc, the city of caves, and the rock on which the later castle was built is honeycombed with them, marking the place as a likely settlement for hunter-gatherer groups. Technically, Nottingham did not become a city until 1897 because it had no cathedral, which was the Medieval requirement for city status.

The name Nottingham is Saxon, ham being the most common form of home or settlement but it was under the Normans that the town came into its own. The conventional way in which William of Normandy controlled the country he had taken by force in 1066 was to build imposing castles, first of timber, later of stone, to overawe the local populace. Nottingham castle was built on top of its natural rock, an extraordinary feat of engineering, in 1068 above the River Lene which was the town's lifeblood. Larger defences were built later, including a twelfth century ditch and bank, widened a century later still and completed with a wall that encircled the town. If the real Robin Hood lived in the area then, he would have seen a rapidly expanding town, with its goose fair and inns like the Bell and Ye Olde Trip to Jerusalem already in existence.

Nottingham was briefly at the centre of the realpolitik of the time when Richard I returned from captivity after the Third Crusade (see Chapter Three) to find the castle in the hands of the local sheriff who was a supporter of Richard's duplicitous brother John. There was a short siege before Richard took it.

Lincoln

The connections with Lincoln are hazier than Nottingham. In many of the Robin stories, the sheriff of Nottingham is the treacherous villain, with or without his 'cousin' Guy of Gisburne, but all

Lincoln has to offer is the outlaw's clothes!

Circular buildings discovered by archaeologists in 1972 prove that the future city (this one *does* have a Medieval cathedral!) was settled in pre-Roman times. The Romans had a legionary base here and called it Lindum. Under the Vikings within the Danelaw it was one of five powerful boroughs which minted its own currency. The castle, high on a promontory overlooking the River Witham, was built in 1068 and the cathedral finished in 1092. An earthquake, very unusual in England and no doubt seen as an omen of God's annoyance, brought it crashing down in 1185. The rebuilt structure, which would have been literally going up in Robin's time, had one of the tallest spires in Europe and the bishop was one of the richest in England, with more monasteries under his control than in any other bishopric. The bishop's palace, part of which still stands, dates from the twelfth century.

Politics hit Lincoln by force in 1141 when the city was caught in a pincer movement between the warring factions of Stephen and Matilda, each claiming to be the rightful ruler of England. Despite this hiccup, Lincoln's wealth continued, based on wool production. The Guild of Weavers was set up in 1130 and specialised in the production of Lincoln Green, a unique colour obtained by mixing *insatis tinctoria* with *reseda luteola* and *genista tinctoria* (dyers' broom) which could be found nowhere else in the country. The result was a bluey-green which, by the way, would not have made for very good camouflage in Sherwood! The first written use of the brand name did not occur until 1510.

Hathersage

Another associated place name in the Nottinghamshire area is in fact further away in the Peak District in what is today Derbyshire. It is reputedly the burial site of Little John, Robin's most trusted lieutenant. In the Norman Domesday survey of 1086-7 it is written Hereseige; by 1220 it was Hauersegg, reminding us of another problem with identifying place names – the lawless spelling of the past!

The present church, probably on the site of an older one, is that of St Michael and All Angels, dating to the fourteenth and fifteenth centuries. At the end of the eighteenth century, a movement grew up among well-meaning amateurs that we usually call antiquarians today. Literary men – and a few women – began to collect historical data from their own areas. They had no access to modern historical research methods and no knowledge of archaeological processes, but they went ahead anyway, usually coming to woefully wrong conclusions. What *is* useful about their work, of course, is that they recorded details that since their time have been lost, so theirs is the only record we have.

Accordingly, in 1780, one such antiquarian, James Shuttleworth, unearthed a tomb in St Michael's churchyard. How he was able to do this is unclear but a thigh bone that he found measured at 28½ inches. Working that out logically, its owner would have been just over eight feet tall! Therefore, in the curious lack of logic that appears in most antiquarians, this had to be the grave of Little John!

Blidworth

For such a small village, Blidworth has it all! It was the setting for the Plough Monday plays, shown in January as an early awakening of spring, not unlike the mummers' plays in which Robin took part. More pertinently, it was allegedly not only the birthplace of Maid Marian, it also has the body of Will Scarlett somewhere in the churchyard.

All the other Robin-associated place names come from Yorkshire and have less currency than their Nottinghamshire counterparts today because the historical background is not so well known or understood (see Chapter Three).

Barnsdale

The early ballads (see Chapter Two) refer to this area as a forest, although dale implies a valley. Today it is part of Yorkshire's West Riding within the Metropolitan Council area of Wakefield, north west of Doncaster.

In the centre of Barnsdale was the village of Hampole where a reclusive hermit, Richard Rolle, lived in the 1340s. He is a shadowy figure, but may have been the first to translate the Bible into English – at the time a heretical thing to do and one which, had it come to light, would have seen him burned alive.

Barnsdale features in two ballads, *A Gest of Robyn Hood* and *Robyn Hood* and the later *Guy of Gisborne* which specifically mention two place names in the area which were settlements within the forest. Various villages along the Roman military road Ermine Street also appear in these texts and if Robin's outlaw band was real, this would have been a target area for unwary travellers.

Within the area today, although its rebuilding on a different site in 1960 has caused problems, stands Robin Hood's Well, designed by the architect John Vambrugh, who built Castle Howard in the same county and Blenheim Palace much further south in Oxfordshire. The original site of the well, between Skelbrooke and Burghwallis, is now under the A1, the Great North Road, which explains its realignment in 1960.

Wentbridge

The village lies alongside the River Went three miles south-east of Pontefract. In the Middle Ages, it was often called Barnsdale because of the forest surrounding it. The bridge itself took the Great North Road over the river and in Robin's time would have been a stone pack-horse bridge, complete with ingles where pedestrians could stand while wagons, carts and the aforementioned pack-horses rumbled past them.

The bridge features in the ballad *Robin Hood and the Potter* – '"Y mete hem bat at Went breg," syde Lytyll John.' The ballad implies that the bridge was a site for wrestling among local lads, reflected in various Robin stories where he fights both Little John and Friar Tuck, ending up in the river both time!

The Sayles

The *Gest of Robin Hood* refers to the Sayles which has been identified today as a plateau overlooking the Great North Road. Again, this is the work of an antiquarian, Joseph Hunter, but the suggestion seems reasonable. As a look-out point for would-be highwaymen, the Sayles was an ideal site. All that is known of the area from the historical record is that its inhabitants were charged by Edward III to contribute to the cost of the knighting of his son, Edward, the future Black Prince, in 1347. Unreasonable as this may seem, it is no different from tax-payers' money being used to refurbish royal houses today!

Campsall

The village in Barnsdale lies seven miles north west of Doncaster and there was a church there, almost certainly wooden with a thatched roof, in Saxon times. The current church, much larger, is Norman and stone-built, the founder being Robert de Lacy, Second Baron Pontefract. A royal charter dating from 1294 gave Campsall the right to hold a market every Thursday and an annual fair that lasted for four days.

The pub the Old Bells, originally the Ring of Bells, is one of the oldest in the country.

In the *Gest of Robyn Hood*, the verse reads:

'I made a chapel in Bernysdale
That seemly is to se,
It is of Mary Magdaleyne
And thereto wolde I be.'

According to legend, the church of St Margaret, as it is today, was the wedding venue of Robin and Marian. As is usually the case, church records do not go back that far.

Abbey of St Mary, York

York was one of the most important settlements in

England for nearly 1,000 years by Robin Hood's time. Under the Romans, it was Eboracum, the base of the VI legion and became Jorvik under the Vikings in later centuries. Strong elements of both these settlements still proliferate in the city which in the Middle Ages was the headquarters of the second richest See in the country, the archbishopric of York, second only to Canterbury.

The Benedictine Abbey of St Mary features prominently in the earlier Robin ballads in which, unsurprisingly, bearing in mind Robin's association with the poor and the accepted avarice of the Catholic church, the abbot is the villain. It was once the richest abbey in England, founded in 1055 and dedicated, as may be expected in the Danelaw, to St Olaf of Norway. Alan Rufus owned the land after the Norman Conquest and granted part of his estate to the abbot and monks of Whitby. The church was refounded in 1088 on the visit of William II and dedicated to the Virgin Mary the following year.

There was a religious dispute in 1132 which lead to a riot before the dissenting group left to found the Cistercian abbey at Fountains. The monks must have felt they had upset God over all this because a fire five years later burned the place down. It was extensively rebuilt between 1271 and 1294.

If we accept the dates ascribed to Robin more recently, that he was operating in the reign of Richard I, the two abbots involved with him would have been Robert de Harpham (1184-9) and Robery de Longo Campo, who was deposed for reasons unknown in 1194. If we take the earlier associated dates from the ballads, then the abbot, between 1258 and 1296, was Simon de Warwick, who oversaw the major rebuilding programmes.

Kirklees

If Little John's grave is believed by some to be in Hathersage, Kirklees convent (in the Middle Ages called a nunnery) is the last resting place of Robin Hood. Kirklees was a Cistercian foundation near Brighouse in Yorkshire, dedicated to the Virgin Mary and St James, Christ's disciple. It was founded by Reiner de Fleming, Lord of Wath-upon-Dearne in 1155.

Between 1306 and 1315, ugly rumours arose concerning the nuns at Kirklees which brought down the wrath of William Greenfield, Archbishop of York, on them. There were stories that three nuns in particular had entertained men, both priests and laity, in their cells. To a celibate church – all nuns were supposed to be married to Christ – this was anathema and the nunnery was watched closely thereafter.

Nevertheless, it limped on until the Dissolution of the monasteries in the 1530s and today relatively little of the Medieval buildings survives. The gate house still stands, along with a barn and part of a farmhouse, itself almost certainly built later from stones taken from the original building

In woods near the River Calder, in what was the nunnery's grounds, is a stone slab that marks the grave of Robin. The legend says that he was taken to the nunnery when seriously ill and nursed by the prioress, who was unable to save him. In his last moments, he called for his bow and fired an arrow out of the open window. Where it landed, that was where he was buried.

Robin Hood's Bay

Firing arrows from windows is a common theme in the Robin stories. Both he and Little John fired from the window of Whitby Abbey, perched high on rocks overlooking the sea. The Bay is a fishing village five miles south of Whitby at the edge of the North York Moors. One of the later ballads has the story of Robin beating off French invaders, pirates who were pillaging the coast, which may have a basis in fact (see Chapter Three). It had been a Viking community about 1000AD and was one of many areas laid waste by William the Conqueror in his harrying of the north in the early 1070s. This systematic destruction, crop-burning and people-killing did considerable damage and was designed to keep rebellious northerners in check. It would be fifty years before the area regained its economic strength.

Robin Hood's Bay was called Baytown until 1544 and is mentioned by the Tudor traveller John Leland at a time when Robin was the focus of the May Day celebrations.

Loxley

There is a tradition in the Robin stories, enhanced by Walter Scott's hugely influential novel *Ivanhoe*, that the outlaw was actually a nobleman, Robin of Loxley (spellings vary) whose lands had been confiscated by wicked Prince John (see Chapter Three).

Loxley Chase, where some claim Robin was born, is a forested area which joined up with Sherwood in the twelfth century. Antiquarian John Harrrison was able, in 1637, to point out to visitors 'Little Haggas Croft wherein is ye foundaccion of a house or cottage where Robyn Hood was borne.'

Monk Bretton

The village near Barnsley was part of a priory founded in the twelfth century by Adam fitzSwain de Bretton. The area is mentioned earlier, before it had ecclesiastic status, as Brettone in the Domesday Book. A Cartulary (document) from the priory, dated the Sunday of Holy Trinity 1322, refers to a land settlement in the area which includes the phrase '... and upon the stone of Robert Hode towards the north'. Recent research into this document has uncovered a mistake; it should actually read 1422, but that is hardly the point. All we have in the Cartulary is mention of a place name, much like the hundreds associated with the outlaw all over the country.

In the end, an evaluation of place names associated with Robin Hood is disappointing. In the absence of any genuine historical record, as opposed to the ballads, all we have is rumour and folklore. Robin is as mischievous and mercurial as his namesake Goodfellow.

Richard Denham

CHAPTER FOURTEEN

WHO WAS ROBIN

HOOD?

Today, Robin stands in Sherwood. He is in his twenties, with fashionable designer stubble, short hair and a duster coat and bandana, more like an outlaw of the American West than a Medieval brigand. His sword (if he carries one) is a lightweight re-enactor's variant of something worn in the fifteenth century. He screams political correctness and is at one with the world of nature exemplified by the forest around him. We never see him kill a deer. His girlfriend, whom he kisses and hugs frequently, rides astride, like a man.

She wears a male doublet and hose whenever she can and is easily Robin's equal in archery, swordplay, forest lore and politics. Little John is a bigger version of Robin, simple, loyal, colossally strong. Friar Tuck is probably in his twenties too. He has a bad haircut, that is not remotely a Medieval tonsure and his curtal robe is a rough-cut version of whatever Robin is wearing. Robin's nemesis the sheriff is probably slightly older. He may have a goatee beard *far* less attractive than Robin's stubble and you would know that, if you asked him, he would be a Brexiteer. His men, sneakily, fire their crossbows with one hand, like a Glock 9mm.

Yes, I am exaggerating, but only slightly. Our image of Robin Hood today stands starkly as created by our own society, as he always has been. And it is just plain wrong. Over the last twenty years, the various movies about Robin have been formed, not in the outlaw's image but against the huge pressure of minority groups who have developed a tyranny every bit as bad as anything the sheriff of Nottingham could have dreamed up. Diversity has meant that Robin must have a black side-kick, hence Azeem, Asneeze and Nazir. He does not feature in *any* of the Robin Hood stories before the film and television versions of our own time. Are we closer to the real Robin now, with these celluloid interpretations? Emphatically not. In fact, we get ever further away. Introduce the artistic element of Manga and Japanese self-defence methods and the whole thing becomes laughable.

Go back half a generation. The celluloid variations of the '80s and '90s paid lip service to the legend (*which* legend we will discuss below). Russell Crowe's 2010 version, Kevin Costner's *Prince of*

Thieves and the now forgotten variant starring Patrick Bergin at least kept a certain verisimilitude. The depiction of a downtrodden Medieval community in *Prince of Thieves*, as shown through Little John and his family was particularly believable, even if their tree-top shantytown was a little bit too Disney theme park.

Go back half a generation more and we are in the realm of the Boy's Own Robin, where politics were straightforward and morality sure. Things were good or bad, personified in the 1950s by the big and little screen Westerns in which the heroes wore white hats and fancy rigs; the baddies were in sombre black. The Robin Hood television series starring Richard Greene was de rigeur viewing for an entire generation. Stories were simple, jokes were obvious, programmes were short (thirty minutes with a break for adverts) and good, of course, triumphed over evil.

The same was true of the Annuals of that period. Robin Hood had been a children's hero by this time for over a century and the genre was comfortable. He was always smiling, not fazed for a moment by having to live in a forest. In fact, for most of the children who read those books, that had an attraction of its own. That generation had no concept of the wandering paedophile (the word barely existed), saw a car only infrequently and spent every summer outdoors with virtually nothing in the way of parental control. 'For Sherwood and liberty!' screams from every page of those much-loved books.

What they describe and what the 1938 Errol Flynn movie showed is a Merrie England that never quite existed, the sun always shone on the dappled glades of Sherwood. Oaks were huge and eminently climbable (except by girls, who were rarely allowed to become Merry Men in childhood games!). The skies were blue and the baddies, hopelessly inept as well as corrupt, always got their just deserts. Look at the studio stills of Basil Rathbone as Guy of Gisborne – he is slimy and shifty. Forget that he was also the brilliant hero Sherlock Holmes; in the 1938 *Robin* he is 100 per cent villain. Now, look at Flynn. Square-jawed, heroic, ramrod-straight, with mischievous sparkling eyes and a ready smile. Was there *ever* a hero as jaunty as his Robin?

To the previous generation, before the advent of moving pictures, the Robin Hood stories were kept alive on both sides of the Atlantic by Howard Pyle. Pyle was writing a humorous prose essay based on a mish-mash of earlier materials, but it is his artwork that keeps the spirit alive. Robin fights with Little John and Pyle is there to paint the scene in dappled sunshine. We can almost hear the clunk of quarter staff on quarter staff and smell the stagnant water under the bridge. When Robin is carried by Friar Tuck over the same water in Pyle's version, look at the Franciscan/Cistercian's face – we just *know* he is going to drop the outlaw right in it.

Earlier artwork is no less fascinating. Daniel Maclise had been commissioned to paint the historical panels in the new House of Commons built after a fire destroyed it in 1834 and five years later he painted a huge canvas 'Robin Hood and his Merry Men entertaining Richard Coeur de Lyon in Sherwood Forest'. The canvas is colourful, in greens, reds and golds. Little John stands to the left hanging up a deer he has just killed. Robin lolls against a tree with a pewter dish on his lap. Will

Scarlett, standing out in red, is making a toast. Richard has just revealed his identity; he has thrown off his cloak and sits in his crusader's white surcoat with the red cross. Dark boughs form a canopy and in the centre, the sunlit greenwood …

Maclise was almost certainly influenced by Walter Scott's *Ivanhoe* of twenty years earlier. There are some books, all of them fiction, that get into the public consciousness and change the game forever. When President Abraham Lincoln met Mrs Harriet Beecher Stowe in 1864, he reputedly said, 'So you're the little woman who caused this great war of ours.' He was referring to her book *Uncle Tom's Cabin* that was a runaway success around the world; Queen Victoria read it four times and wept every time. It told the story of a vicious slaver owner, Simon Legree, who mistreats his slaves, especially the eponymous hero. Mrs Beecher Stowe had never seen a slave, knew no slave owners and let her schmaltzy, melodramatic style run riot. Around the world, millions believed that *Uncle Tom* was hard fact; it was not. Generations later, Harper Lee's *To Kill A Mockingbird* painted a similar unforgiving picture of the deep American south, albeit in a later era, being packed with racism. Seen, as the story is, through the eyes of a child did not alter the basic message. Isaac Asimov's *I, Robot* deals with a fear that is actually growing today. Man has created Artificial Intelligence but cannot control it. The machines are taking over. We are all going to die. But on the way to that dearth, according to John Wyndham's *Midwich Cuckoos*, we are all going to be infiltrated with aliens, at first in the guise of beautiful, identical, golden-eyed children. And Peter Brenchley's *Jaws* put the cause of marine biology back for years. Not only were Great White Sharks unstoppable murderers of humans, they were probably in any stretch of water near *you*!

Ivanhoe was perhaps the first of these. It established beyond recovery that Robin Hood lived in Sherwood, that he was of knightly birth and that he lived in the reign of Richard the Lionheart. None of this was true, any more than *all* slaves were brutalised, children were aliens or Great Whites will get you, but it became part of the cultural heritage anyway. The important point about *Ivanhoe* is that it was written not for children, but for adults, adding to the believability of Robin Hood. This was not Pokemon, or Mario, In the Night Garden or Muffin the Mule, clearly children's entertainment. This made it *just possible* that Robin was real.

Before Walter Scott penned *Ivanhoe*, his friend Joseph Ritson collected the tales of Robin Hood and tried to analyse them. Francis Child in America did a fuller job of it years later, but it was Ritson who took the broken fragments of the damaged ballads and turned the outlaw into a fully-fledged freedom fighter, a meme which has never gone away. With his own liberal attitudes and opposition to the tyranny of the *ancient regime*, Ritson merely substituted the sheriff of Nottingham and King John for the governments of Britain and France. Robin was the American colonists, taxed without representation in the English parliament. He was also the *sans-culottes*, the starving peasants who stormed the Bastille prison in Paris in 1789. July 4 and July 14 could both have been Robin Hood's days.

We find the *real* Robin Hood's days in a much earlier period. The First of May was the ancient beginning of spring, the Celtic Beltane and the country people of Tudor England celebrated the fact with dancing around maypoles, hitting each other with sticks and producing Robin and Marian as King and Queen of the May. The Puritans did not approve, because, other than a dour obsession with the Bible, they did not approve of anything and it was they who effectively made Robin and the greenwood disappear for half a century.

And finally, in our reverse search for the truth, we come to the ballads, both the later examples from the seventeenth century and the earliest from 200 years before that. The ballads are infuriating not just because they are anonymous, largely undated and damaged, with lines and verses missing, but because they tell us so little about our hero. Marian is not there. Neither is Tuck. Only three Merry Men are listed – Little John, Will Scarlett and Much, the miller's son. Some tales are set in Sherwood, others in Barnsdale. There is little continuity. This Robin clearly despises the Church, the greedy bishops and abbots at the top of the ecclesiastical hierarchy. Yet he accepts (in the later ballads) the 'curtal friar' into his band. He loses as many duels as he wins and even archery, for which he is renowned, is not always successful. Little John is clearly a better shot.

But the huge question mark about the ballads, our earliest written records of Robin Hood is; what were they based on? Sloth in *Piers Plowman* knows the rhymes of Robin Hood (1377) but none of the written ballads go that far back. There must therefore have been an oral tradition – songs and stories told around the campfires about … who?

Can we find a *real* Robin in recorded history, someone who gave birth to the legend? The central theme of Robin Hood today, that he stole from the rich and gave to the poor, can be found nowhere. There is not a single instance of any criminal anywhere who did that; it flies in the face of human nature.

We have looked already at the outlaw gangs of the Middle Ages – the Tuddenham-Haydons, the Folvilles, the Cotterels. It is conceivable that Robin *may* have his origins among them, but the name does not occur. What is consistent in the earliest ballads is social status. Robin is not a knight, still less Earl of Huntington. He is a yeoman. And so, according to most experts, were the bulk of the audience who listened to the ballads; Robin was one of them. The problem with this is the definitions of social standing were changing all the time, as economics changed and peoples' perception changed with it. To take an extreme, and late, example, a yeoman in the nineteenth century was a cavalry soldier belonging to a local unit, usually raised in the 1790s, for defence 'of hearths and homes'. This is very different from the meaning applied, say, to the thirteenth and fourteenth centuries, but it has similar origins. *Villein* disappeared during the Middle Ages, although village survived and with a different spelling came to mean baddie, evil person. Likewise, the Saxon *ceorl* had gone by the early twelfth century but as 'churlish' has been retained for sullen, oafish behaviour. The common theme is one of contempt from people of superior rank.

From 1413, when a law called the Statute of Additions required anybody involved in a lawsuit to state their rank, yeomen appear between gentlemen (above them) and husbandmen (below). These class distinctions were not fixed and one vital element in English society, as opposed to European, is that *in theory*, with luck and hard work, a man could climb the social ladder. In France, he could not. There, there were three estates – the Church, the aristocracy and everybody else. The French suffered three revolutions in sixty years; the English, none. Another piece of legislation was brought in earlier, in 1363; the Sumptuary Laws, which stipulated the kind of clothes a person wore. Yeomen could spend up to 40 shillings (£2) a year; husbandmen 26 shillings and gentlemen 70 shillings. Those who doubt that kings, from Henry II to Henry VIII presided over a police state should look at these laws in detail.

By the time the ballads were being printed, the term yeoman had become very wide. It was harnessed by royalty in the creation of yeoman archers, as in the retinue of Edward IV in the 1470s. The 'beefeaters' who guard the Tower of London are officially the Yeoman Warders. This dual role, of servant and yet free man, probably existed throughout the Middle Ages. The *Black Book* of 1472 lists the duties of royal yeomen and one of these is to be 'yeoman of the bowes for the king'. Such men were chosen for their 'manhoods, shotyng and specially of vertuose condicions'. In other words, they were 'good yeomen' in the sense of Robin and his Merry Men. The other meaning was of small landowner, although exactly what that means in terms of land value and yearly income varies enormously.

Geoffrey Chaucer's yeoman in *The Canterbury Tales* (1386) works for the knight and his son the squire. His coat and hood are green. His arrows, sharp and bright, have peacock feathers. He carried a huge bow and a sword and buckler, with a leather brace on his left forearm to protect it from the stinging bowstring. He carries a horn and knows a great deal about woodcraft. And then, with that typical sly humour for which Chaucer is renowned – 'A forester was he, smoothly [truly] as I guesse'. He *sounds* and *looks* like Robin Hood, but he has no name.

Three Scottish writers, Andrew de Wyntoun, John Fordun and Walter Bowers, all wrote about Robin over a twenty year period in the early-mid fifteenth century. 'Then arose the famous murderer, Robert Hood'. As we have seen, 'then' meant 1266 and the possibility that Robin fought for the rebellious earl Simon de Montfort against Henry III. The problem is that these were *Scots* writers, not English and they were writing nearly 200 years after the events they wrote about. Whatever their original sources were is now unknown.

Joseph Hunter, the antiquarian, tried to pin Robin down to the royal progress made by Edward II between April and November 1323. Although that sounds very precise, Hunter based the premise on finding the name Robert Hood as a porter of Edward's chamber in the same period and another one, married to Matilda, from Wakefield. The fact that nothing criminal is known about either of these men should have given Hunter pause for thought, but he was an antiquarian, not an historian and went on to make ever blinder assumptions.

Searches for the name Robin Hood are fruitless. There are actually several of them and more are being found all the time. By the thirteenth century, even the surname Robinhood exists. A Gilbert Robynhood lived in Sussex and is mentioned in tax returns for 1296. Katherine Robynhood was probably the daughter of Robert Hood, a councillor for the Vintry in London in 1294.

Can we find any *criminal* Robin Hoods? Yes, we can. Robert Hood murdered Ralph of Cirencester in a garden in that town in 1214. Robert Hood was a man on the run in York in 1226. Alexander Robehod was wanted for theft in Essex in 1272. Robert Robehod was a sheep stealer in Hampshire. William Robehod was part of an outlaw gang operating in Berkshire in 1261-2. Any of these – and there are more – *could* be the origin of the legend. William Robehod is the most likely. The gang consisted of three men and two women (oddly) who were suspected of harbouring fugitives as well as highway robbery and had run from the law, hence their description as outlaws. From the record, it looks as though William's real name was Robert le Fevere and Robehod was just a nickname. In the end, this most hopeful of cases peters out. Why should the sordid story of a *Hampshire* thug become enshrined in heroic exploits involving anti-clericalism and archery from *South Yorkshire*? In today's small world of instant and worldwide communication, that would not be a problem, but in the thirteenth century, such a link is almost impossible.

Perhaps, in time, a record will come to light which makes such a link, so that in future books we will read a single line – 'the folk hero Robin Hood, based on ??? of ??? in the year ???' Until then, all we have is a fascinating collection of informed guesswork, but it makes our search for Robin worthwhile.

'My name is Robin Hood of Barnesdale,' the outlaw says in *Guy of Gisborne*, 'a fellow thou hast long sought.'

We are seeking him still.

Select Bibliography

Anglo-Saxon Chronicle
Ashley, Mike, *British Kings and Queens,* Robinson, 2014
Baigent, Michael and **Leigh, Richard,** *The Temple and the Lodge* Arcade, 1989
Blakemore Evans, G., *Elizabethan-Jacobean Drama,* A&C Black, 1989
Dobson, R.B. and **Taylor, J.,** *Rymes of Robyn Hood,* Alan Sutton 1989
Duffy, Eamon, *Saints and Sinners,* Yale University Press, 1997
Embleton, Gerry and **Howe, John,** *The Medieval Soldier,* Windrow and Greene, 1994
Folklore, Myths and Legends of Britain, Readers' Digest 1973
Fraser, George MacDonald, *The Hollywood History of the World,* Michael Joseph, 1988
Fraser, George MacDonald, *The Steel Bonnets,* Pan Books, 1979
Girouard, Mark, *The Return to Camelot,* Yale University Press, 1981
Guest, Ken and Denise, *British Battles,* Harper Collins, 2000
Harvey, John, *The Plantagenets,* Fontana, 1967
Holt, J.C., *Robin Hood,* Thames and Hudson 1989
Hussey, Maurice, *Chaucer's World,* Cambridge University Press, 1967
Keen, Maurice, *The Outlaws of Medieval England,* Routledge, 1961
Mortimer, Ian, *The Time Traveller's Guide to Medieval England,* Vintage Books 2009

Norwich, John Julius, *The Popes; a History*, Vintage Books, 2012

Orme, Nicholas, *Medieval Children,* Yale University Press, 2001

Plowden, Alison, *Elizabethan England,* Readers' Digest 1982

Ross, Anne, *Pagan Celtic Britain,* Constable 1992

Sharp, Mick, *The Holy Places of Celtic Britain,* Blandford Press, 1997

Vansittart, Peter, *Green Knights, Black Angels,* Macmillan 1969

Weir, Alison, *Britain's Royal Families,* Pimlico, 2002

Weir, Alison, *Elizabeth the Queen,* Pimlico, 1999

Wills, Chuck, *Weaponry,* Carlton Books, 2006

Other titles by BLKDOG Publishing that you may enjoy:

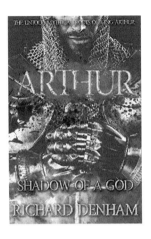

Arthur: Shadow of a God
By Richard Denham

King Arthur has fascinated the Western world for over a thousand years and yet we still know nothing more about him now than we did then. Layer upon layer of heroics and exploits has been piled upon him to the point where history, legend and myth have become hopelessly entangled.

In recent years, there has been a sort of scholarly consensus that 'the once and future king' was clearly some sort of Romano-British warlord, heroically stemming the tide of wave after wave of Saxon invaders after the end of Roman rule. But surprisingly, and no matter how much we enjoy this narrative, there is actually next-to-nothing solid to support this theory except the wishful thinking of understandably bitter contemporaries. The sources and scholarship used to support the 'real Arthur' are as much tentative guesswork and pushing 'evidence' to the extreme to fit in with this version as anything involving magic swords, wizards and dragons. Even Archaeology remains silent. Arthur is, and always has been, the square peg that refuses to fit neatly into the historians round hole.

Arthur: Shadow of a God gives a fascinating overview of Britain's lost hero and casts a light over an often-overlooked and somewhat inconvenient truth; Arthur was almost certainly not a man at all, but a god. He is linked inextricably to the world of Celtic folklore and Druidic traditions. Whereas tyrants like Nero and Caligula were men who fancied themselves gods; is it not possible that Arthur was a god we have turned into a man? Perhaps then there is a truth here. Arthur, 'The King under the Mountain'; sleeping until his return will never return, after all, because he doesn't need to. Arthur the god never left in the first place and remains as popular today as he ever was. His legend echoes in stories, films and games that are every bit as imaginative and fanciful as that which the minds of talented bards such as Taliesin and Aneirin came up with when the mists of the 'dark ages' still swirled over Britain – and perhaps that is a good thing after all, most at home in the imaginations of children and adults alike – being the Arthur his believers want him to be.

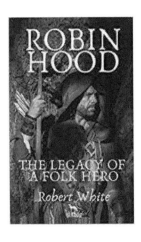

Robin Hood: The Legacy of a Folk Hero
By Robert White

If you thought you knew about Robin Hood... then think again!

Written by Robert White, chairman of the World Wide Robin Hood Society.

Many tales have been told about Robin Hood. The traditional stories of good versus evil and his quest to regain his rightful inheritance are universally appealing. The legend has intrigued generation after generation and everyone has their own personal vision of Robin Hood - a swashbuckling hero; a romantic outlaw; a bandit thief; a fighter of injustice or a benevolent champion of the people. Numerous books have been written by historians trying to untangle the myth, establish his actual existence and speculate on just who he might have actually been. Consequently, the subject of the globally renowned hero of English folklore has become extensively complex but the observations included in this publication should provide a brief overview of some of the key facts, issues and perceptions surrounding Robin Hood.

Robin Hood: The Legacy of a Folk Hero gives a

fascinating insight into the numerous aspects of one of the world's most enduring and iconic legends. Robert White discusses interesting facts and titbits surrounding the outlaw, and then reflects on how the Sherwood Forest hero has become a global phenomenon who, over 800 years, evolved into 'the people's champion'. Embark on an journey from the legend's mythical roots to how, across the ages, the tales of Robin and his merry men has developed in many diverse ways that still impact us to this   day.

Whatever your opinions and beliefs, this title will reveal just why Robin Hood has become so much more than simply a mythical outlaw of English folklore.

Weirder War Two
By Richard Denham & Michael Jecks

Did a Warner Bros. cartoon prophesize the use of the atom bomb? Did the Allies really plan to use stink bombs on the enemy? Why did the Nazis make their own version of Titanic and why were polar bear photographs appearing throughout Europe?

The Second World War was the bloodiest of all wars. Mass armies of men trudged, flew or rode from battlefields as far away as North Africa to central Europe, from India to Burma, from the Philippines to the borders of Japan. It saw the first aircraft carrier sea battle, and the indiscriminate use of terror against civilian populations in ways not seen since the Thirty Years War. Nuclear and incendiary bombs erased entire cities. V weapons brought new horror from the skies: the V1 with their hideous grumbling engines, the V2 with sudden, unexpected death. People were systematically starved: in Britain food had to be rationed because of the stranglehold of U-Boats, while in Holland the German blockage of food and fuel saw 30,000 die of starvation in the winter of 1944/5. It was a catastrophe for millions.

At a time of such enormous crisis, scientists sought ever more inventive weapons, or devices to help halt the war.

Civilians were involved as never before, with women taking up new trades, proving themselves as capable as their male predecessors whether in the factories or the fields.

The stories in this book are of courage, of ingenuity, of hilarity in some cases, or of great sadness, but they are all thought-provoking - and rather weird. So whether you are interested in the last Polish cavalry charge, the Blackout Ripper, Dada, or Ghandi's attempt to stop the bloodshed, welcome to the Weirder War Two!

Click Bait
By Gillian Philip

A funny joke's a funny joke. Eddie Doolan doesn't think twice about adapting it to fit a tragic local news story and posting it on social media.

It's less of a joke when his drunken post goes viral. It stops being funny altogether when Eddie ends up jobless, friendless and ostracised by the whole town of Langburn. This isn't how he wanted to achieve fame.

Under siege from the press, and facing charges not just for the joke but for a history of abusive behaviour on the internet, Eddie grows increasingly paranoid and desperate. The only people still speaking to him are Crow, a neglected kid who relies on Eddie for food and company, and Sid, the local gamekeeper's granddaughter. It's Sid who offers Eddie a refuge and an understanding ear.

But she also offers him an illegal shotgun - and as Eddie's life spirals downwards, and his efforts at redemption are thwarted at every turn, the gun starts to look like the answer to all his problems.

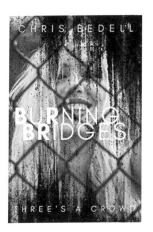

Burning Bridges
By Chris Bedell

They've always said that three's a crowd...

24-year-old Sasha didn't anticipate her identical twin Riley killing herself upon their reconciliation after years of estrangement. But Sasha senses an opportunity and assumes Riley's identity so she can escape her old life.

Playing Riley isn't without complications, though. Riley's had a strained relationship with her wife and stepson so Sasha must do whatever she can to make her newfound family love and accept her. If Sasha's arrangement ends, then she'll have nothing protecting her from her past. However, when one of Sasha's former clients tracks her down, Sasha must choose between her new life and the only person who cared about her.

But things are about to become even more complicated, as a third sister, Katrina, enters the scene...

Father of Storms
By Dena Jones

Imagine losing everything you loved as well as the future you'd wished for so long to come true.

Seth was born with the gift to manipulate energy, unfortunately his skills mark him as a target for one who wishes to control everything. So began a life running from those who would seek to command him, a life that spans over a thousand years waiting for the day when all will be once again as it was.

Captured in modern day London, Seth needs the help of his companions, the Mara, to show him who he is through dreams of his past, so he can save the family he has waited so long to have. A warrior bred for battle must fight once more but this time the battlefield is his mind. Can Seth win, or will he finally lose who he is and become the weapon of the man who started his nightmare all those years ago? *Father of Storms* is a story told through time, a tale of love and hope where there seems to be none and above all it is a reminder that if you believe, truly believe then even from the darkest places, good things come to those who wait.

www.blkdogpublishing.com

Made in the USA
Columbia, SC
30 August 2020